The Song of the Wind in the Dry Tree

The Song of the Wind
in the Dry Tree

Commentaries on Dogen's *Sansho Doei*
and Koun Ejo's *Komyozo Zanmai*

REI RYU PHILIPPE COUPEY

Translated from the French by Rosemary Cottis

HOHM PRESS
Chino Valley, Arizona

Cover design: Zac Parker
Interior design and layout: Becky Fulker, Kubera Book Design

Translated from the French by Rosemary Cottis.
Originally published as *Le chant du vent dans l'arbre sec.* ISBN 978-2-910677-94-7
© Arkanorum, 2011
Editions Charles Antoni / L'Originel
25 rue Saulnier, 75009 Paris, France

Library of Congress Cataloging-in-Publication Data

Coupey, Philippe, author.
  [Chant du vent dans l'arbre sec. English]
  The song of the wind in the dry tree : commentaries on Dogen's Sansho doei and Koun Ejo's Komyozo zanmai / by Rei Ryu Philippe Coupey ; Translated from the French by Rosemary Cottis.
     pages cm
  Includes bibliographical references and index.
  ISBN 978-1-935387-82-4 (alk. paper)
  1. Dogen, 1200-1253. Sansho doei. 2. Ejo, 1198-1280. Komyozo zanmai.
3. Meditation--Buddhism. I. Title.
  BQ9449.D654S233313 2014
  294.3'85--dc23
                                          2014013489

HOHM PRESS
PO Box 4410
Chino Valley, AZ 86323
800-381-2700
www.hohmpress.com

This book was printed in the U.S.A. on recycled, acid-free paper using soy ink.

I dedicate this book to my master, Taisen Deshimaru.

I would like to thank Jonas Endres, Jantje Hannover,
Christoph Martin, Frank Tatas, Agnès Villette,
Juliette Heymann, Jean-Pierre Romain,
Marie-Pascale Meunier for their help.

Contents

Preface

The teachings given here by Philippe Coupey, Zen master in the lineage of Taisen Deshimaru consist of commentaries on two 13th century Japanese texts, the *Sansho Doei*, a collection of poems composed by Dogen Zenji between 1245 and 1253, and the *Komyozo Zanmai* written in 1278 by his disciple and successor, Koun Ejo.

Before going any further, let us remember that reciting and commenting on the "sayings of the elders" is a style of practice that the Zen school has fostered from its earliest days. It remains the best method for transmitting the fundamental teachings and for bringing the tradition to life, constantly renewed. For, in fact, the same words, the waters of the same spring, act as a vehicle for all of the individual voices which, in whatever times or under whatever skies, speak to us of the authentic experience of the Way. This is how this fresh interpretation should be taken: as the resonance of an intimate and fundamental experience which, beyond space and time, is addressed to our heart, shedding light on our own quest and ratifying the discoveries that we may have made along the way. Clearly, then, this is a message that is not intended to come under the heading of scholarship or to add to our intellectual baggage, but to enrich our spiritual life. "For words can be effective if they come from the non-personal, from the non-self, and if they are listened to and heard by the non-self," explains Philippe Coupey in his commentary on the *Komyozo Zanmai*.

Dogen, the founder of the Soto Zen lineage in Japan, is known today mainly for his magnum opus, the *Shobogenzo*, or *Treasury of the Eye of the True Law*, in which he sets out his understanding of the teaching and practice of the patriarchs, an understanding that his Chinese master, Tendo Nyojo (T'ien-t'ung Ju-ching) certified before sending him back to Japan to establish the authentic practice of the Way. The poems of the *Sansho Doei* are less well known. Nevertheless, they constitute a rich facet of his work, more accessible than the *Shobogenzo*, which is a work so dense, paradoxical and laced with coded references that it is sometimes disconcertingly impenetrable to the point where, without the necessary tools, only a handful of the élite can elucidate its mysteries. The *Sansho Doei* reveal another aspect of the master's thought, certainly also present in the *Shobogenzo*, but crystallized here to a pure state: his poetic sensitivity set entirely in the immediacy of experience and stripped of all didactic, polemic or doctrinal concerns.

But let there be no misunderstanding; if Dogen's poems refer to nature in the first instance, nonetheless, they speak of the experience of awakening at every opportunity, for, as Bernard Faure tells us, "Nature [for Dogen] is not a concept, but concrete reality perceived from the point of view of awakening: the world of awakening itself." And later, as Faure explains, "The nature of which Dogen speaks is nothing like nature in ordinary language; it is nature in awakening, in the 'direct experience' that antecedes any distinction between subject and object."[1]

Dogen, in this approach to reality, conforms to a tradition that is deeply rooted in Japanese poetry, particularly in *haiku*, whose ambition is simply to express, in the clearest and purest terms, the "silent coinciding" that in the grace of the moment puts an end to all separation between our experience, our presence in the world, and reality as it is, the "ineffable" reality of which Dogen speaks in the chapter of the *Shobogenzo* entitled "Inmo."

Zen Master Philippe Coupey is clearly aware of all of this. "Even if the poems [of the *Sansho Doei*] refer to nature, to landscapes, seashores, the passing of springtime, and so on," he tells us, "it is always consciousness that is the subject. Free, natural, ordinary consciousness that is neither *for* nor *against*."

Coupey has taken from the collection twelve poems on which to comment, and he gives a reading of them that is always pertinent – a result of the intimate understanding that he has of his subject, of the simple fact that he draws from the same well: a long, profound experience of the practice of zazen. This experience is often original, demonstrating a mind that is free and in perfect harmony with the natural order of things. Surely poetry, and especially the poetry of pure intuition that Dogen in particular and Zen in general produce, should be reappropriated and to some extent reinvented by the reader to whom it is addressed. A passage from this book serves to illustrate the freedom and richness of interpretation that Philippe Coupey demonstrates.

In his commentary on Dogen's line, *"What words can express the inexpressible beauty?"* he states that, "Consciousness is more vast than the cosmos," and adds, "Neither the expert in Buddhism, nor the painter, nor the scientist can truly transmit this. But the poet, even if he cannot express it, at least manages, like Master Daichi or Master Dogen, to preserve and contain it. That which can neither be indicated nor displayed can still be preserved." So the poet is established among those who guard the secret! This places the bar very high for all those who attempt to practice the art of poetry.

As for the *Komyozo Zanmai*, this is a pure jewel, which, in Philippe Coupey's eyes, as in mine, encapsulates and exudes the purest essence of transmitted Zen. In evidence we have this phrase that leaves nothing unsaid: *"If you abandon yourself to the exhalation and let your inhalation fill you in a harmonious coming and going, nothing remains but a zafu beneath the empty sky, the weight of a flame."* We find, in the sayings of the elders, a number of blinding truths like this one, able to pierce the thickest defenses to strike the heart of man and there give a lasting ring to the bell of awakening.

Koun Ejo, as we have said, was the disciple of Dogen, who transmitted the dharma to him and made him his successor. Here we touch on an important and delicate point in Zen. Zen rests on two pillars: practice and transmission, intimate experience and certification. Zen is only truly present when these two facets are united in one person. This is doubtless true of many ways and traditions, but Zen stresses it more than the others do, to the point where there is a genealogical tree that goes back from patriarch to patriarch, from master to master, all the way to the historical Buddha. In the case of Philippe Coupey, the line comes from Taisen Deshimaru and, through him, goes back to the founders, passing through Kodo Sawaki, Dogen and all those who preceded them: Wanshi, Fuyo Dokai, Gensha, Tozan, Sekito, Yoka Daishi, Eno, Sosan, to name just a few of the masters who have made an indelible impression on the neurons of our lineage, whether it be through their writings or through the anecdotes that have passed into our collective memory. Leaving aside the formal aspect of this transmission and the certificate, duly stamped, that has accompanied it in recent times at least, it is worth asking ourselves the question: What is it that has been transmitted?

"The teaching [given] in the 13th century," writes Philippe, "was absolutely no different from that which we, as Zen disciples, have received and are in turn transmitting today." A little later he explains, "We can see that through the centuries nothing has been added or taken away." But what is this "real thing" that is transmitted? "Perhaps it is the Way, awakening; the inner joy that one cannot express to others. Love – we must each decide for ourselves what is the real thing," he tells us, in answer to his own question.

We could continue on this theme endlessly. But I would like to express the profound emotion that I feel, carrying me forward and encouraging me to persevere, when I find flowing from the pen of Philippe Coupey the same lessons in life that I draw untiringly from the texts of the founders, the same basic, vital simplicity that comes as close as can be to the "real thing," the "*that*" of the Zen masters: "When we eat, when we go to the toilet, when we sleep, when we go to bed – whether or not we go to bed alone – it is always with the mind of zazen." And further, "It is not a question of whether or not we are progressing, but simply of not following our thoughts. This doesn't mean behaving like a robot, but exactly the opposite: not being driven by phenomena, by this or that, because by going from thought to thought we will only find ourselves trapped against the railings in the end."

That is a passage that perfectly echoes Kodo Sawaki: "Something that is fascinating about Dogen Zenji is how he saw the Buddha-dharma as the self, instead of simply putting out fairy tales for ordinary people. For example, he talks about the vehicle of the single Buddha: Amithaba, Shakyamuni and ourselves as one Buddha. And for him, the practice of zazen itself is spreading the

Buddha-dharma – not building temple halls or pagodas. Dogen Zenji's zazen is a completely transparent zazen. It's of no use to ordinary people. *'Don't practice the Buddha-dharma for yourself. Don't practice to make a name for yourself. Don't practice to profit from it. Don't practice to have spiritual experiences. Only practice the Buddha-dharma for the sake of the Buddha-dharma.'* [*Gakudoyojinshu*] That's his Buddha-dharma."[2]

Since we do not practice for ourselves, what impact can it have to let thoughts pass as Deshimaru urges us to do? "I think," says Philippe Coupey, "that it has had an effect on everyone – on ourselves, on the people in the street, in the city. Today everybody says it, even psychiatrists. And little by little it will spread until suddenly, one day, the whole population will be saying it and perhaps we will all speak the language of Zen." Why not, since we are all children of the same crystal-clear truth? "Let the marvel come," Meister Eckhart tells us.

One final thought in conclusion. The Buddha-dharma is nothing other than the practice; in other words, the intimate experience that each of us has of reality. But we have seen that there is also transmission, which is nothing but the authentication of this direct experience from generation to generation. The sayings of the elders play a key role in this. They are the lighthouses and beacons without which navigating our way would be very dangerous, and as such they constitute a precious form of transmission. "Constantly reading and rereading, that is how the Way should be studied," writes Zen monk Philippe Reiryu Coupey. It is in this sense that I strongly recommend reading and attending his teachings.

Luc Boussard
April 2010

Painting of Eihei Dogen by Reikai Vendetti, Zen monk.

PART I

Sansho Doei

Introduction

Dogen's *Sansho Doei* is a long series of poems (approximately sixty verses in total), almost all written at Eiheiji, which at the time was no more than a small isolated mountain hermitage. Master Dogen began writing this collection in September 1245, one year after he and his disciples settled at Eiheiji. The last of the poems was composed in August 1253, a few weeks before his death. Yet, the *Sansho Doei* was not published until 1747 by Master Menzan Zuiho.

Sansho means umbrella pine. It was also an old name for Eihei mountain where Dogen had his hermitage beneath the umbrella pines. And *Doei* means the song of the Way. So *Sansho Doei* is *Songs of the Way of the Umbrella Pine*.

Most of the poems in the *Sansho Doei* are dedicated to the Shogun of the time, Hojo Tokiyori. He was originally a samurai who, in the 13th century, ended up taking charge of the empire. He was also a disciple of Dogen, who had given him bodhisattva ordination.

At that time, the way of the samurai and the way of Zen were mutually influential. Why? Simply because the samurais practiced zazen alongside monks, creating ties and strong relationships. This interdependence is well known. Many masters composed poems and other texts dedicated to samurais, for example Daichi Sokei's poems to Kikuchi[1] or Dogen's for Tokiyori, yet many more spoke equally directly about samurais. In any case, it is interesting to note the delicacy and sensitivity of these poems, even though they were dedicated to warriors.

The poems of the *Sansho Doei* are very clear and easy to understand; for the most part, they are obvious observations. Even if they refer to nature, to landscapes, seashores, the passing of springtime, and so on, it is always consciousness that is the subject – free, natural, ordinary consciousness that is neither *for* nor *against*.

Twelve Poems From the *Sansho Doei* *

By Master Dogen

Translated by Master Taisen Deshimaru

---

* The numbering of the poems corresponds to the order chosen by the author.

ONE
The waves die out on the shore.
The light wind holds its breath.
The abandoned boat gently drifts.
In the silence of the night,
The moon in the depths of the firmament
Spreads her peaceful light.

TWO
On the russet leaves of the long winter month,
The spotless snow softly sparkles
Under the moon's rays.
What words can express the inexpressible beauty?

THREE
Wherever it may go, from wherever it may come,
The waterbird erases its traces
But never loses its way.

FOUR
When it dives or when it is carried by the rolling wave,
Who can tell the seagull from the mandarin duck?

FIVE
Where is our native village deep in the mountains?
Where should we seek it?
Our native village is where we are living, here and now.

SIX
Our mind is colorless.
Nobody can see it.
It is just like the dew or the frost...

SEVEN
Oh! my little hermitage, where I am hibernating
Amid the clouds, the ice and the snow…

EIGHT
No one is unsettled by the swift passage of the days
Nor disquieted by the running of the horse
Galloping after the sun…

NINE
The inner intoxication of our mind
Is like the autumn sunset over the forest
Where the woodcutter works.

TEN
The flowers bloom in the spring storm
And from the foot of the mountain, their perfume rises.

ELEVEN
In the grassy dojo of my hermitage,
Summer has arrived.
We put on the light kolomo
And lower the reed blinds.

TWELVE
Springtime is coming to an end.
It passes, even if we want to hold it back,
Even if we regret its passing...

Commentary

ONE

The waves die out on the shore.
The light wind holds its breath.
The abandoned boat gently drifts.
In the silence of the night,
The moon in the depths of the firmament
Spreads her peaceful light.

This is perhaps one of the most beautiful poems of the *Sansho Doei*. When we read, for example, the first two poems of the *Eiheikoroku*, also by Dogen,[1] we can see that the difference between these two collections does not lie in the profundity of the text, but in the images and metaphors used, as well as in the tones and rhythm of the verses – even though we are obviously dealing with a translation.

This first poem talks of the *bonno*, illusions, and the way in which they vanish during zazen when we realize their true nature is without foundation and therefore illusory. *Bon* means that which troubles or disturbs; and *no*, that which causes suffering, torments. If we take desire as an example, it is not desire in itself that causes suffering, but the attachment that it produces.

When we consider the living world in general, cosmic life, we can see that *bonno* do not truly exist. It is in the human world that they appear. But it is also in precisely this human world that they can also disappear.

The waves die out on the shore.
The light wind holds its breath.
The abandoned boat gently drifts.

In this poem, as in most Zen poems, the waves represent the anxieties, uncertainties and passions that come and go. And the abandoned boat is the abandoned ego. The boat is empty...there is no longer any consciousness that could be described as "you" or "me." Without "you," without "me," it is *ku*, empty consciousness, conscious emptiness; the inside is empty.

The abandoned boat gently drifts.

This "inside is empty" is the first of the twenty *ku* or, in Sanskrit, the twenty *sunyata*. Buddha explained what these twenty *ku* are in the Mahayana sutra, *Prajnâ Paramita*. They are difficult to understand. The second of the twenty *ku* says that the outside is empty. The outside represents existence face to face with the six senses; we might also say "opposed to" the six senses, in other words opposed to "me," to "you."

So the inside is empty, the outside is empty. This is the abandoned boat.

And the fourth of the twenty *ku* tells us that emptiness is empty. Emptiness, *sunyata*, is a concept, "our" or "your" concept. And so it is always "something." Let's destroy this concept – we could say this final concept – to which we could continue to cling, and then nothing will remain in existence but the reality of things, or in short, reality.

To make reality more accessible, more graspable, we say: reality is zazen.

In the silence of the night,
The moon in the depths of the firmament
Spreads her peaceful light.

In these last three lines, the moon, the symbol of harmony, represents awakening. No eyes can disturb its light. Silence and light, even at midnight, are the essence and also the symbols of Soto Zen.

That's what zazen is. It is the wind that does not move, the still mind. It is the abandoned boat that no longer belongs to anybody. To talk of an "empty" boat is a good image, but the word "abandoned" is even more accurate. For "abandoning" is an action rather than a state of mind; it is a decision, it is the act of detachment. It is like a *koan* or even like a vow. It is unconscious faith.

The wind has dropped. The waves, illusions, anxiety have calmed, for there is no owner anymore…the boat is abandoned. In the depth of the night, only the moon illuminates the landscape.

The waves die out on the shore.
The light wind holds its breath.
The abandoned boat gently drifts.
In the silence of the night,
The moon in the depths of the firmament
Spreads her peaceful light.

TWO

On the russet leaves of the long winter month,
The spotless snow softly sparkles
Under the moon's rays.
What words can express the inexpressible beauty?

Scholars of literature and poetry say that Zen poetry – Dogen's or Daichi's, for example – is not real poetry, and that it is vastly inferior to poetry as they understand the term; one could even say, inferior to literature itself. This is because Zen poetry *carries a message*, a teaching that lies behind the words, while for them "real" poetry does not convey any message at all; with a few exceptions, it simply glorifies nature, while capturing passing phenomena in imagery.

Here, then, is a poem, which at first glance seems to be poetry without a goal, transmitting no message but that of pure poetry. But between the lines, Dogen is in fact saying much more. He composed this poem at Eiheiji, in the mountains in the north of Japan. Snow has fallen and the moonlight is shining in the long winter night. It is very beautiful.

Snow on the russet leaves: snow, here, represents *ku*, emptiness; the russet leaves represent *shiki*, phenomena; and all of this is shining under the rays of the moon. But we can also read it as saying that the snow (*ku*) and the leaves (*shiki*) are not different in the end. *Ku* becomes *shiki* and vice versa. *Ku* can also mean non-form. In Zen we have the following famous phrase: *ku sokuze shiki, shiki sokuze ku*, non-form becomes form and form becomes non-form.

On the russet leaves of the long winter month,
The spotless snow softly sparkles
Under the moon's rays.
What words can express the inexpressible beauty?

During the long winter months, the snow-covered leaves sparkle in the moonlight. How can that be explained? Why should it be? There is no point in talking about emptiness as if it were separate from phenomena. There is no need to create opposition – whether it be in an attempt to understand a poem or in our daily lives. Having said that, if you want to decode a Zen poem to grasp its message, look first for symbols for *ku*, emptiness and *shiki*, phenomena. Then you will understand right away.

Of course, this is beautiful. But what is beautiful? It is not the snow that is beautiful. It is not the leaves that are attractive. It is not the moon that touches us so deeply, but everything together. It is our life in the sangha, it is our life in zazen, at work, with our families; it is our life on this earth that is beautiful, as long as we do not make a separation between "me" and "others," which however, certainly does not mean that we are all identical or that there are no differences between us.

What words can express the inexpressible beauty?[1]

The expert in Buddhism cannot explain it, the artist cannot paint it and the scientist cannot measure it. Yet today, modern science manages to measure everything: the speed of consciousness, the speed of light. And through their telescopes, scientists have arrived at a conclusion identical to the teaching of Zen and of Buddha: consciousness is more vast than the cosmos.

So neither the expert in Buddhism, nor the painter, nor the scientist can truly transmit this *inexpressible beauty*. But the poet, even if he cannot express it, at least manages, like Master Daichi or Master Dogen, to preserve and contain it. That which can neither be indicated nor displayed can still be preserved.

Snow covers the russet leaves in the moonlight. Hidden by the snow, seen by the moon…in the end, what is this *inexpressible beauty*? It is neither one thing nor two things.

THREE

Wherever it may go, from wherever it may come,
The waterbird erases its traces
But never loses its way.

This poem is one of the best known from the *Sansho Doei*.

Let things pass. Let your thoughts pass, and what you see, and what you hear, and what you feel. If you do not stay stuck on anything – a sight, a smell, a word – you can be concentrated on all things. This is zazen.

This question of letting things pass is certainly not exclusive to Zen. It is also found in the practice of martial arts. In martial arts, it is a question of being concentrated-not concentrated in order to disable the adversary, while in Zen, it is being concentrated-not concentrated in order to be available at any moment. We never used to hear Master Deshimaru say, "Ah, no, I'm busy right now," or "Oh, I have too much work to do!" He was always available.

This is what it means not to leave traces.

Wherever it may go, from wherever it may come,
The waterbird erases its traces
But never loses its way.

Of course, if the waterbird never loses its way, it is because it follows neither the southern route nor the northern route. Why? Because there is no north or south.

Many Zen stories say the same thing, but not always in the same way. For example, a monk asked Master Joshu, "Why did Bodhidharma come to China?"

And Joshu replied, "The oak tree in the garden."

This has the same meaning, the same dimension as Dogen's poem, but it is not on the same level.

Or again, another monk came to see Joshu and asked him, "I have come with nothing, *mu*. What should I do in this situation?"

"Throw it away," Joshu replied.

"But I just told you that I came with nothing. What do you want me to throw away?"

"In that case, get rid of it quickly!"

Again, this is the same thing.

Master Nansen asked a question of some of his disciples who were arguing about a cat. It was a question that was difficult to answer – a *koan*. But that didn't matter. Nansen asked the question all the same, then added, "If you can't answer my question, I will cut this cat in half!" Of course, nobody was able to reply…and Nansen killed the cat.

Soon afterwards, his first disciple, Joshu, came along. Nansen, after repeating his question, asked him, "If you had been there, what would your reply have been?"

Joshu took off one of his sandals and put it on his head.

"Well, it's a pity you weren't there today. You would have saved the cat's life."

All of these stories have the same meaning. It is not a question of morality; it is not a question of good or bad. It is the bird that comes and goes but leaves no traces and is never lost.

Wherever it may go, from wherever it may come,
The waterbird erases its traces
But never loses its way.

Commentary

These days our intuition has become very weak, particularly because of the development of our cerebral cortex. Our "outer brain," the cortex, has become so developed that it has eclipsed our "inner brain," the hypothalamus. This may be why we have so much trouble understanding *koans* and stories like these today. But through the practice of zazen, we can rebalance these two brains; that is, we can let the cortex (the cognitive and intellectual function) rest for a few minutes or a few hours each day. And little by little, through this practice, we can awaken and give life to our inner, intuitive brain, the one that leaves no trace and never loses its way.

21

FOUR

When it dives or when it is carried by the rolling wave,
Who can tell the seagull from the mandarin duck?

This poem is much shorter than the others and much less well known.

We are always subject to ups and downs. When we find ourselves in these states, we think we can tell, but in fact we can never tell one thing from another, not even a seagull from a duck. It's satori or illusion. It could be either one. It all depends on our attitude, our state of mind in the moment; and so it is sometimes one, sometimes the other.

When it dives...

In other words, when we dive into the cave of the black mountain.*
This could refer to *kontin*, the state of drowsiness, inner fog.

...or when it is carried by the rolling wave

When we are floating on the waves and everything becomes buoyant; we feel satisfied, happy, although we might be in *sanran*, the state of agitation.

During zazen we should stop doing *everything*. Master Deshimaru even said, "Stop imagining; stop observing!" This is the profound meaning of these lines.

---

* Or more accurately, in the words of Master Tozan, "the demons of the black cave."

At the time when Deshimaru made this comment, "stop observing," I didn't take much notice because I thought that, on the contrary, we needed to observe all the time. Much later, I said to myself, "Okay, we shouldn't observe external things, we shouldn't be constantly looking around us at other people or our surroundings, but instead we should observe ourselves, always ourselves." But if that's what it means, why is it considered so profound?

Still, profound or not, this is really the point: to stop observing means to observe neither the outside nor the inside.

In the 8th century, Master Ha-shang Mahayana – that was his name – was the first person to introduce Buddhism to Tibet.[1] He was a Zen (*Chan*) monk and in Tibet, he became a master. He founded a dojo in Lhasa and settled there. This was before Tibetan Buddhism, Lamaism, developed in the country. Before that time, Zen had existed but it had not been there for very long. However, in the end, the Tibetans asked Ha-shang to leave. They didn't understand his mind and they literally threw him out. Anyway, Ha-shang said one day, "Whatever thoughts may arise, we should not examine them, whether they are apparent or not."

No phenomenon should be examined. This is the deep meaning of those words of Ha-shang's and these lines of Dogen's.

When it dives or when it is carried by the rolling wave,
Who can tell the seagull from the mandarin duck?

FIVE

Where is our native village deep in the mountains?
Where should we seek it?
Our native village is where we are living, here and now.

"I want to live in the mountains…" "I want to live by the sea, or perhaps in the countryside…" "And I want to live in the sun, on a far-off island…"

We always hear people saying, "I want, I want…" But for whom do I want? I want for myself. And later, it's, "I want for God, for Buddha…" and obviously, while we're at it, I also want *satori*!

So where is our native village? Where is true religion, the true practice? Do we need to go to Japan or India to find them?

There is no need to go anywhere: we are already there.

In my commentaries on the poems of the *Eiheikoroku*,[1] also written by Dogen, I talk a lot about *sanko*, which means "living in the mountains, living in the forest." Living in the mountains or in the forest also implies settling in a peaceful place, as, for example, during a *sesshin*.* *Sanko*, going into the forest, is in the end no different from sitting down under the Bodhi Tree. So *sanko* means zazen, because it is not only a question of place, but above all, of mind.

---

* To participate in a *sesshin* is to practice meditation (zazen) with other people in a quiet place for several days.

Sanko also means *do not be led by the mountains or the forest.*
Not only *do not be led*, but do not even be influenced or tainted
by them. Do not be tainted by the Bodhi Tree. Do not be tainted
by your environment. It is pointless to be influenced by our
environment because, in the end, the environment is nothing but
our greater body.

There is no need to go looking for Buddha in your foot or *satori*
in your hand, not to mention your mind. "I want to meet Buddha."
That is a misunderstanding. Buddha and I are not in duality. There
are not two but one: no separation. That is the meaning of this
poem.

Where is our native village deep in the mountains?
Where should we seek it?
Our native village is where we are living, here and now.

Everything exists here and clearly now: the mountain, the Bodhi
Tree, *satori*. So why should we want to go to Bodh-Gayâ to sit
under the Bodhi Tree, as many Americans do today? There are
even organized tours during which you can spend a few moments
sitting under the tree (for a high price, I guess!)

The Bodhi Tree cannot be anywhere other than where we are.

SIX

Our mind is colorless.
Nobody can see it.
It is just like the dew or the frost...

Our mind or spirit has no form. Not only does it have no form, but it is also invisible. We often say, "That person has a good mind." But in reality, the person who has a good mind is one who has no mind: *mushin*. Neither good nor bad, neither black nor white, neither red nor blue. True mind, at least in Zen teaching, is when phenomena become *ku*, emptiness.

True mind is *colorless*; it is invisible, formless. Why? Because it rests on nothing. It flows like the water in a river. It is perpetually changing, so one cannot give it a name or stick a notice on it that says, "Here is mind." Like the constantly flowing water, it goes everywhere and it becomes cloud, it becomes rain, it becomes dew, frost; it becomes ice, tears. Even pus is just water in the end, and that water is a symbol of *ku*, emptiness.

Yet our original mind, like our original nature, does not change. That which is perpetually changing does not change: *ku sokuze shiki, shiki sokuze ku*. Emptiness, non-form, becomes form and form becomes non-form.

Our mind is colorless.
Nobody can see it.
It is just like the dew or the frost...

This poem has two meanings. The first is that, in its normal condition, mind has no particular form. The second is that everything returns to *ku*, to emptiness, to water. Everything becomes dew; everything becomes frost.

These three lines also describe the mind during zazen: *hishiryo*. *Hi*: beyond; *shiryo*: thought. During zazen, we practice "beyond thought," "thinking-not thinking."

Our mind *is just like the dew or the frost...*

SEVEN

Oh! my little hermitage, where I am hibernating
Amid the clouds, the ice and the snow...

This is a poem that talks of zazen and the mind of zazen. It is very short: two lines.

The *little hermitage* where Dogen is hibernating is the square meter within which one sits when one practices the posture of zazen. It is the square meter where he sits and where his *zafu*, kimono, *kolomo* and *kesa* are. It is where the "form" of a man, woman, god or goddess sits – "form" because it is not only Master Dogen who sits there but the whole world. It is not an individual; it is not somebody who goes from thought to thought.

This Dogen form is hibernating. *Hibernating* here, means staying far from society, apart, in solitude: that is zazen. In zazen, in a dojo, there may be twenty or thirty of us and yet each of us is completely alone. Alone on a zafu, where no desire exists any more. There is nothing, everything is stopped – stopped-not stopped. At that moment everything becomes *hishiryo*, beyond thought, unconsciously, naturally and automatically.

True *sesshins*, the *sesshins* that are important in the eyes of masters like Dogen and others, do not take place in summer but in winter. Master Deshimaru called the summer camps that we practiced at the temple of La Gendronnière and elsewhere, "spiritual vacations." (He even insisted on this being printed on the publicity leaflets.) But he never said that about the *sesshins* that took place in winter, in the snow and the cold.

The mind of zazen is cold. This does not mean that Zen lacks compassion or warmth, but simply that the mind is not drawn to the right or the left by the passions, thoughts or individual karma.

Amid the clouds...

This is the mind of zazen, the mind that passes, without stopping on any point, without following its thoughts or becoming their prisoner. It is *hishiryo*, beyond thought. It is thinking-not thinking. It is the symbol of true freedom and of the mind that is not preoccupied by its desires – sex, love, fame, money or even life. It is not a question of life and death. No, it is simply the mind that, resting on nothing, becomes true mind.

Clouds are also a symbol of *ku*: emptiness.

The meaning of this poem is that we must go beyond all things.

Oh! my little hermitage, where I am hibernating
Amid the clouds, the ice and the snow...

EIGHT

No one is unsettled by the swift passage of the days
Nor disquieted by the running of the horse
Galloping after the sun...

No one is unsettled by the swift passage of the days...

Everybody understands that time passes quickly, but most people do not face up to the reality of this. They bury it under a heap of activities, far from their awareness. And yet, this suppressed awareness makes them suffer. Everybody says, "Oh, time passes quickly!" but that's all; the observation stops there.

Nor disquieted by the running of the horse
Galloping after the sun...

The horse runs after the sun. The sun runs in the sky. And we too run right up to the coffin.

It/us: that's the meaning of this poem. However, I do not think that everybody runs. Some people stop, observe themselves, concentrate, seek the truth. But there are not many of them. Kodo Sawaki, in his commentary on the *Shodoka* said, "You who practice and seek the truth are great ones."

Seek the truth. Doing zazen, we can realize that this truth, *the* truth, exists only in the body, here and now.

NINE

The inner intoxication of our mind
Is like the autumn sunset over the forest
Where the woodcutter works.

Here is a poem that appears to be a simple observation. This *inner intoxication* that Dogen mentions is not, of course, due to alcohol but to our illusions – the illusions of our weakened awareness – to our mistakes, our narrow mind, our weaknesses; we could say our deep instincts.

At first, in infancy, we want immediate satisfaction of our desires; this begins at the mother's breast. Then, as adults we start to want, for example, power over others. Our deep instincts may be different, such as the reproduction of our own genes, the natural selection of the species, and so on.

Therefore, if there is such a thing as progress, it does not involve *overcoming* our instincts but *transforming* them through zazen practice.

Nor does this *inner intoxication* concern drugs – even if it could be said that, in a way, a drug is also an illusion. It is true that hallucinogens (LSD and other similar drugs) can bring about joy – or let's say, a state of expanded consciousness. But it is time-limited, because these states of "paradise" are only artificial, as Baudelaire proclaimed.

That kind of drug – I say "that kind" because what is *not* a drug? – carries dangers for the hypothalamus, which is weakened by hallucinogens. Through the practice of zazen, on the other hand, we strengthen the hypothalamus more and more. The chemical activity in the hypothalamus during zazen is very different from the chemical activity in the hypothalamus of somebody who is taking hallucinogens or other drugs because, unlike drugs, the practice of zazen brings us back to the normal condition, the original condition of humanity.[1]

After taking drugs, one quickly becomes tired, and of course, one is soon disappointed and sad. One also feels a great loneliness. Yet after doing zazen, one is neither dissatisfied nor lonely.

However, this is not the case for the woodcutter in this poem who, alone in the forest, looks at the autumn sky feeling lonely and even melancholy. Master Deshimaru explained that, "The mind of our inner intoxication in this world is just like the melancholy of the autumn dusk for the woodcutter." This dusk is an image representing those who are bound in the chains of illusion.

> **The inner intoxication of our mind**
> **Is like the autumn sunset over the forest**
> **Where the woodcutter works.**

TEN

The flowers bloom in the spring storm
And from the foot of the mountain, their perfume rises.

Everything changes, whether it is the body, the mind, plants, nature or the environment. Our environment seems to be in increasing upheaval. Sometimes in mid-January it seems like the middle of spring: the trees are in bud, plants are flowering, butterflies are flying about and the birds arrive from Africa too early thinking that spring is already here. Other species of birds have not yet left as they should have...and yet it seems clear that the temperature will soon drop. Even the bears are perturbed; they wake up from hibernation much too soon.

As for human beings, they are perturbed as well, and not only because of financial matters, of course – how to react, what attitude to adopt in the face of one problem or another – but also because the North and South Poles are disappearing. The polar ice caps have shrunk by forty percent in the last decade. We are panicking because we are losing our points of reference, our habits. In the final analysis, it is our lives that are endangered: our families' lives, our country's, our civilization's – and mostly because of human stupidity.

The flowers bloom in the spring storm
And from the foot of the mountain, their perfume rises.

Here is another, very different translation of these two lines.*

> The catalpa bows down
> In the spring storm.
> It begins to flower.
> From top to bottom of the mountain
> The soft scent of its perfume spreads.

Here, instead of "flowers," we have a catalpa, a tree with highly scented white and yellowish flowers that blooms in May.

In these two lines, Dogen is telling us that in spring, flowers open after a storm. Phenomena occur at their appointed time. There is no need to panic. We could simply say: good fortune becomes misfortune; misfortune becomes good fortune. And this alternation is constantly repeating.

---

* By Jacques Brosse, *Polir la lune [Polishing the Moon]*, Albin Michel, 1998.

ELEVEN

In the grassy dojo of my hermitage,
Summer has arrived.
We put on the light **kolomo**
And lower the reed blinds.

Here, again, we have a simple observation rather than a poem.

Among other things, we must follow the cosmic order by marking the change from one season to another, which is always done in temples and monasteries.*

We put on the light **kolomo**...

The monk or nun's robe is not the same in winter as in summer. In winter, we wear a thicker robe, in summer, a lighter one. The same is true of the *kesa*.

And lower the reed blinds.

In Japan, in Dogen's time, the dojo was protected from the cold in winter by thick cotton curtains, which were replaced in summer by light reed blinds. Yet we continue to practice zazen anyway, whether it is summer or winter.

Those who practice do not worry too much about wearing fashionable clothes. They don't try to change their appearance or focus on the proprieties, but just try to practice zazen and live

---

* At La Gendronnière Zen Temple, for example, a *sesshin* takes place at each change of season.

simply. When we are ordained, we receive the *kolomo*. This means that we are abandoning all that is superfluous. If we wear the *kolomo*, kimono or *kesa*, even if it is just for one zazen, during that zazen we give up all decoration.

For beginners, it's fine to wear pants for zazen. But it's better not to wear jewelry, makeup or perfume. In daily life people are always wanting to change their appearance: the cut of their clothes, their size, pants that are baggy or pleated, and so on. People today are constantly changing their look, their posture.

Regular practitioners, as well as monks and nuns, are like everybody else. But at the same time they do not change at all over the centuries: always the same robe in the same color, always the same *kesa*, whether it is made of thick wool or light cotton.

For them, wearing the robe, the *kesa*, is also a way of saying that they renounce their former life and what they used to be. It is also "being an example." For certain people, it is very easy. They arrive and right away they get hold of a kimono, or even a *kolomo* – although the *kolomo* can be expensive. But for others, it is more difficult. The first time that I wore a basic kimono, I didn't feel very comfortable. It felt a little like wearing a dress. I wasn't used to it. However, the important thing is that it makes zazen more comfortable. The feet rest on the bare thighs, on the skin.

Wearing the robes and with shaved heads, people look very much the same. This is something that you notice very quickly when you practice zazen: there is no real distinction, and no separation, neither from the people with whom you practice, nor from anybody else. When we practice zazen in this way, we practice with the whole world.

TWELVE

This is the last poem that I will comment on. It is a very simple poem, like all those in this collection.

> *Springtime is coming to an end.*
> *It passes, even if we want to hold it back,*
> *Even if we regret its passing...*

We often say, "Time is money." But time is much more than that. We can always get money. Even if we can't do it this time around, we can always become rich in a future life if that is what we really want. Strong desires have influence and transmigrate forever. If we have not gotten what we want today, tomorrow we will be able to get it.

Yet, this is not true of time. This poem talks about time and impermanence – the passage of time. We cannot get time back once it has gone, and this is the case right up to the end, whether we like it or not. But the problem with time is that this implies "running after" it or "running away" from it. Or, as the poem explains "wanting to hold it back" and, if it gets away, "regretting" it. This is the world of *bonno*, illusions.

We could spend all our lives in this "*bonno* world." However our teaching, our practice, is always to continue straight ahead without interruption as if we were alone on the earth, as one master said. I think that what he meant by this was not to be distracted by what we see with the eyes, what we smell with the nose, what we hear with the ears, but on the contrary, to go ahead without interruption, even in our sleep.

The fact is that we do not have the choice, since everything is changing, anyway. That is why we must concentrate on each point of our lives so that all the points together form a harmonious line.

And these poems of Master Dogen's *Sansho Doei* do just that: they introduce a harmonious line into our lives, even if, like this poem, they are no more than a gentle breeze announcing the beginning of the end of spring.

> **Springtime is coming to an end.**
> **It passes, even if we want to hold it back,**
> **Even if we regret its passing...**

Painting of Koun Ejo by Reikai Vendetti, Zen monk.

PART II

Komyozo Zanmai

Introduction

The *Komyozo Zanmai* is a text by Dogen's great disciple and successor, Koun Ejo, who is known for the tremendous support that he gave to his master, both as his secretary, scribe and editor of the whole of the *Shobogenzo*, and also as the person in charge of Dogen's dojo (which at the time was a small dojo named Eiheiji*), thus allowing his master the time to develop the profundity of his teaching.

It was in 1278, twenty-five years after the death of his master, that Ejo composed the *Komyozo Zanmai*, "the essence of *satori*." Or according to Kodo Sawaki, it is "the essence of the *Shobogenzo*." This is the only text that Ejo wrote during his lifetime.

Master Deshimaru translated and then commented several times on this short text, notably at the Pernety dojo in May 1981, the year before his death. He liked it a great deal, as did his master, Kodo Sawaki,† and he studied it regularly, constantly reading and rereading – that is how the Way should be studied.

---

* Today Eiheiji is the principal temple of Soto Zen in Japan. To say "small dojo" is a little ironic [Editor's note].

† The *Komyozo Zanmai* was the last text that Kodo Sawaki commented on at the end of his life.

43

I remember that at the time during 1981-1982, the teachers who went to lead sesshins in France and Spain would read the *Komyozo Zanmai* from start to finish during zazen without any commentary at all. They must have thought that anybody could understand Ejo's words without trouble, although it is not really that easy to comprehend.

To grasp this text, we need to understand the word *komyo*. *Komyo* is light, illumination, the light that makes the shadows of ignorance disappear; and *zo* is the warehouse, storehouse, granary. *Zanmai* means samadhi, awakening or, if you like, *hishiryo*, consciousness. So we could say that the *Komyozo Zanmai* is "the samadhi of light in the storehouse" or "the granary (i.e., the mind) illuminated by samadhi." This is zazen practice: the spiritual power of non-acting in the light of *mushotoku*, the light of non-goal, the light that lights up by itself. It is the place where the light of wisdom breaks through ignorance and shines on reality.

Ejo also uses the word *komyo* to mean the essence of religion. And with this meaning of *komyo*, *komyozo* can embrace our whole lives and bring us happiness and freedom. This is mind connected to the whole cosmos – which is nothing other than the normal condition of our mind.

KOMYOZO ZANMAI

BY KOUN EJO

Translated by Master Taisen Deshimaru

I feel a great respect from the depths of my compassion for you who continue the practice of zazen in the state of mind that I will now describe: without grasping anything or having any goal, without being influenced by your personal understanding, without letting the experience that you have acquired in the dojo make you arrogant. With all the energy of your body and mind, throw them totally into *komyozo*, without looking back at time.

Do not seek *satori*. Do not try to listen to *mayoi*, illusory phenomena.

Do not hate the thoughts that arise, do not love them either, and above all, do not nourish them. In every way, you must practice the great sitting, here and now. If you do not nourish a thought, it will not come back by itself. If you abandon yourself to the exhalation and let your inhalation fill you in a harmonious coming and going, nothing remains but a *zafu* beneath the empty sky, the weight of a flame.

If you have no expectations about what you are doing and refuse to consider anything, you can cut everything off through zazen alone. Even if the eighty-four thousand *bonno* come and go, if you attach no importance to them, then, right then and there, from each one of them, one after the other and all together, the marvelous mystery of the storehouse of great wisdom can arise.

There is not only the *komyo* of the time of zazen. There is also the *komyo* that, step after step, action after action, gradually shows you that each phenomenon can be realized immediately, automatically, independently of your own understanding and your personal thoughts. Such is the true and authentic certification that exists without disturbing the expression of *komyo*.

It is the spiritual power of non-acting in the light that illuminates itself. This *komyo* is originally non-substance, non-existence. This is why, even if many buddhas realize it in this world, they are still not of this world. And being in nirvana, they are however not there either.

At the hour of your birth, *komyo* was not in existence.

At the hour of your death, it will not disappear.

From the point of view of the buddha-state, it does not increase.

From the point of view of the senses, it does not diminish.

Just as when you have illusions or doubts, you cannot ask the right question, when you have *satori*, you cannot say so.

Moment by moment, do not consider anything according to your personal consciousness. Twenty-four hours a day, you should be as calm and supremely tranquil as the dead. Do not think of anything by yourselves. Thus, from breath to breath, your profound nature, like your sensory nature, will unconsciously, naturally become non-knowing, non-understanding.

From that point, everything can naturally become calm, the radiance of *komyo*, in the unity of body and mind. That is why when we call it, it has to reply quickly. It is the one and only *komyo* that harmonizes the people of *satori* and the people of illusion in one whole. So even if you start moving, the movement should not disturb you. And the forest, the flowers, the blades of grass, animals, human beings, all phenomena – be they long, short, square or round – can be realized immediately, automatically, independently of your personal understanding and the personal activity of your thoughts.

Do not become attached to clothes, nor to food, nor to your home. Do not succumb to sensual desire or to the attachment of love, which are like the activity of animals. There is no point asking others about *komyo*, because their *komyo* cannot be of any use to you.

At its origin this samadhi is the holy dojo, the ocean of all the buddhas. It is therefore the greatest and most holy of all the seats transmitted directly from buddha to buddha through the holy universal practice. Being disciples of Buddha now yourselves, you should do zazen peacefully on his seat.

Do not sit on the infernal *zafu*, the *zafu* of the *gaki*, animal or *asura*, nor on the *zafu* of the *shomon* or the *engaku*. And do not practice anything but *shikantaza*. Do not waste your time. This is what is known as the authentic spirit of the dojo and the true *komyozo* samadhi, the marvelous and splendid *satori*.

This text should only be read by true disciples of Dogen, those who have permission to enter his room.

I have written it for my companions in zazen so that they will not hold mistaken points of view, as much to improve myself as to educate others.

Commentary

This is how the *Komyozo Zanmai* begins:

I feel a great respect from the depths of my compassion for you who continue the practice of zazen in the state of mind that I will now describe: without grasping anything or having any goal, without being influenced by your personal understanding, without letting the experience that you have acquired in the dojo make you arrogant. With all the energy of your body and mind, throw them totally into komyozo, *without looking back at time.*

...without grasping anything or having any goal...

Here Master Ejo describes the exact mind of zazen, the mind without goal – *mushotoku*. The teaching that he gave in the 13th century was absolutely no different from that which we, as Zen disciples, have received and are in turn transmitting today.

Master Deshimaru always used to bring up this question, talking about *mushotoku*. *Mu* means "non" and *shotoku*, profit, or to obtain.

The very first thing that I heard from his mouth during zazen when I began practicing at the Paris dojo in 1972, was the word *mushotoku*. "Here in Soto Zen," he explained, "there is nothing to obtain."

For example, do not think that through your zazen practice you are going to achieve good health, or the energy you would like to have so that you can get through more tasks, be more effective at work, more well-balanced at home, or in short, that you are going to become a little happier. It is a mistake to think that one can obtain all this through zazen. If someone is in that state of mind, they are just following their own ego, projecting zazen on zazen. They are just becoming attached, standing still.

Nor is there any need to be hung up on your posture. In the dojo we do not get hung up on anything, not on anything that relates to our perspective or our personal well-being. Ejo is telling us something very important: we must go further than our own health, our own well-being. Go beyond.

Through *mushotoku* we can understand non-discrimination and obviously non-separation. But of course we cannot function like this in society, where it is necessary to have a goal. However, even then we are certainly *not* not-*mushotoku*, that is to say, *ushotoku* – even in business. We are free of attachment to success or failure. Thus, even living in the city, we can, through *mushotoku*, protect *komyozo zanmai*, the light of non-goal.

...without being influenced by your personal understanding, without letting the experience that you have acquired in the dojo make you arrogant.

That is, without showing any superiority because of your position as a monk or nun, your knowledge of Zen, your length of practice, or the regularity of your attendance in the dojo. Here is a great *bonno*, illusion! Who does not possess, at least from time to time, a contentious mind, specifically, a mind that compares and so creates separations? Who does not do that? Who does not think themselves better than others or – the same thing – worse than others?

It is important that Dogen said that we must always consider ourselves to be only halfway along the path. We are only halfway along the path, all of us, including Dogen himself. This is the mind of *shoshin*, beginner's mind, the mind of the beginning. "You are not even halfway along the path!" This is stream-entering – *sotapanna*, in Sanskrit, one who enters the current, enters the Way. You should always be one who is entering the Way.

With all the energy of your body and mind, throw them totally into komyozo, without looking back at time.

Throw your whole body and mind into *komyozo*, the light of awakening. And do this with all your energy. Do it without looking back or ahead, towards the past or the future. This is what it means to open up completely to the present moment, where there is no comparison, no relativity, because all is here – body and mind. Then *komyozo*, the marvelous light, appears.

Do not grasp, do not be grasped, do not color things with your personal understanding, do not be proud. Right now, with all you possess, plunge into the Way without hesitation, without looking up, down, left or right, without spending time gazing at the side of the road.

The monk, the nun, the true practitioner must forget everything, at every moment. Not becoming stupid or forgetful, but simply not stagnating. Not stopping, not dwelling on things, but always in motion. Of course this does not mean traveling, or looking at other things – we already look too much, there is no need to be looking all the time – but simply to keep our lives moving, like a river. The river does not travel, it *is*.

But it is better to start now than later. Because as we grow older it is sometimes difficult not to stagnate in one's practice, difficult always to go, go, always to give, give… and not just receive. Giving, transmitting the dharma, teaching non-fear unconsciously, by one's presence. Giving is the same as *going*. It is *going* toward others, helping them in their practice, helping them on the Way. Helping to lessen our original common suffering. It is impossible always to receive; it is necessary, indispensable, to give what we have received and what we continue to receive.

Do not seek satori. Do not try to listen to mayoi, illusory phenomena.

Do not hate the thoughts that arise, do not love them either, and above all, do not nourish them. In every way, you must practice the great sitting, here and now. If you do not nourish a thought, it will not come back by itself. If you abandon yourself to the exhalation and let your inhalation fill you in a harmonious coming and going, nothing remains but a zafu beneath the empty sky, the weight of a flame.

Do not seek satori. Do not try to listen to mayoi, illusory phenomena.

Ejo wrote this text in the 13th century and today we are teaching exactly the same thing. Nothing has changed. Nothing ever changes. We are born, we have children, we work, we are happy, we are unhappy, then we die… and what has changed? Nothing.

Do not seek satori, awakening, or you will never know that it is the vast consciousness of zazen. Do not listen to *mayoi*. *Mayoi* means illusions. It is the certification of all phenomena. Do not spend your time certifying phenomena, or even studying them.

Do not hate the thoughts that arise, do not love them either, and above all, do not nourish them.

When grasping and rejecting are abandoned, the vast consciousness appears.

Recently some Zen texts were found in the Chinese caves of Dunhuang.[1] One of them is entitled, *The Gate of Immediate Entry to Chan*, written by the Zen monk Ha-shang Mahayana during the Tang dynasty. The posture of zazen is described – the position of the back, the knees pressing the ground, the chin tucked in, and so on. Ha-shang also writes about the eyes and the way that we should look-not look in the dojo and during zazen. All of this description dates from 1300 years ago. Ha-shang also often repeats, "Do not follow your thoughts!" It is the same today. We describe the posture exactly as he described it and we are always saying, "Do not follow your thoughts!" So we can see that through the centuries nothing has been added or taken away – except for a few new rules, which are certainly necessary, and a few more ceremonies.

In that text, Ha-shang also talks about *mushin*, no-mind, just as we do today in our zazen practice by describing it as non-examination. "Whatever thoughts may arise, we should not examine them, whether they are apparent or not. No phenomenon, whatever it may be, should be examined." This is not a question of psychology, which is something that only concerns the ordinary person. Ha-shang and the masters of transmission are speaking to practitioners of the great sitting that is zazen; they are speaking to the disciples of Buddha. Therefore, non-examination is never taken to mean, "We are free and we can do whatever we want," – absolutely not – but rather, "We are free to do what we have to do." This is no different from what Ejo wrote later in Japan, or from what we say today in the dojos here in Europe.

> *So, do not seek **satori**. Do not try to listen to **mayoi**, illusory phenomena. Do not hate the thoughts that arise, do not love them either, and above all, do not nourish them. In every way, you must practice the great sitting, here and now. If you do not nourish a thought, it will not come back by itself.*

Some people hate their thoughts – it is true that they can be a massive, useless burden. But be content not to consider them. They are not important. Let them pass. This is something that we endlessly repeat in the dojos, every day, four times a day, the whole year 'round. "Let your thoughts pass, do not follow your thoughts." Master Deshimaru said it constantly.

I think that it has had an effect on everyone: on ourselves, on the people in the street, in the city. Today everybody says it, even psychiatrists. And little by little it will spread until suddenly, one day, the whole population will be saying it and perhaps we will all speak the language of Zen.

But in order not to follow one's thoughts, it is necessary neither to chase nor to flee.

If you do not nourish a thought, it will not come back by itself.

No cause, no effect. This is not something New Age, but rather something rigorous, abrupt. All through this short text Ejo affirms that we must plunge without hesitation and without doubt into *komyozo zanmai*, always going ahead without turning back.

If you abandon yourself to the exhalation and let your inhalation fill you in a harmonious coming and going, nothing remains but a zafu beneath the empty sky, the weight of a flame.

The first time that I heard or perhaps read this sentence a long time ago, I was very impressed. I copied it out and pinned it to the wall. It is from this empty sky and this flame in triangle form, like the posture of zazen, that vast consciousness can appear.

Nen means flame and *to* means candle, so *nento* is candle flame. *Nento* is also the name of Nento Butsu, one of the buddhas of the past, before Shakyamuni Buddha. Nento Butsu is the buddha that appears in our daily lives, particularly through our sight, hearing, sense of smell, and so on. It is said that *nento* is true nirvana realized through our whole body.

If you have no expectations about what you are doing and refuse to consider anything, you can cut everything off through zazen alone. Even if the eighty-four thousand* bonno *come and go, if you attach no importance to them, then right then and there, from each one of them, one after the other and all together, the marvelous mystery of the storehouse of great wisdom can arise.

In the words of the master, "Refuse to consider obstacles, mistrust them. Do not have anything in common with anything at all. Do not take anything into serious consideration. If a thought arises, take no notice of it." Not taking anything into serious consideration means, for example, *even if the eighty-four thousand* bonno *come and go*, do not act according to these thoughts. Let them go. Leave these thoughts to themselves. And then, from each of these thoughts, from each of our thoughts, will arise the *komyozo zanmai* of the great wisdom *hannya*.

If you have no expectations about what you are doing and refuse to consider anything, you can cut everything off through zazen alone.

Here, of course, Ejo is talking about the mind during zazen that gradually soaks into daily life outside the dojo. If you refuse to consider anything and you live in harmony with your breathing, you can cut everything off just through the posture of zazen, *shikantaza*.

Cutting everything off is not something to be sad about. On the contrary, it is when the Way embraces our whole lives and brings us happiness and freedom. It is said that when you cut through thoughts in the rhythm of the inhalation and exhalation, you can abandon all things. And it is only when you do nothing that you can do all things. If you refuse to consider things consciously, then you will be natural, automatically rejecting your body and mind.

Master Ejo tells us: do not consider anything; in this way you can cut through your karma – your bad karma – *our* bad karma, because if you do not consider anything at all, nobody considers anything at all.

It is certain that sustaining our thoughts has a tendency to make the meditation period shorter. However, if you do that, the brain, far from becoming clear and simple, becomes even more complicated. If you become attached to a particular thought or if you continue to go from thought to thought, the devil arises.* So do not argue with these dualistic thoughts, do not become the devil's partner or you will no longer be able to progress or even to exist. Of course, if you follow your breath during zazen, if you constantly come back to the posture and if you listen without listening to the *kusen* [the oral teaching], you cannot keep a thought going for very long. Then where will the devil be?

So, even if the eighty-four thousand *bonno* arise and fade away, from the moment when we absolutely refuse to consider them, giving up the pursuit of thoughts, our mind becomes pure. Here, pure means "without anything." Our egoism disappears, and from each of those thoughts, the *komyozo* of the great wisdom, the light of awakening, will be able to arise.

The last sentence of this paragraph of the *Komyozo Zanmai* intrigued me. Here is part of it:

---

* The devil is that which gives rise to dualistic thoughts such as, "This is right; that is not right," and so on.

...then and there, from each one of them** [them: the bonno, the thoughts], **one after the other and all together, the marvelous mystery of the storehouse of great wisdom can arise.

This can be understood thus: if we stop our cerebral machinations, all things are then no more than one single body.

*There is not only the **komyo** of the time of zazen. There is also the **komyo** that, step after step, action after action, gradually shows you that each phenomenon can be realized immediately, automatically, independently of your own understanding and your personal thoughts. Such is the true and authentic certification that exists without disturbing the expression of **komyo**.*

*There is not only the **komyo** of the time of zazen.*

Do not forget that *komyo*, translated as light, illumination, is not just any light, but the one that emanates from *hishiryo*, consciousness (*hi*, beyond; *shiryo*, thought). *Komyo* is the invisible but brilliant light that exists not only during zazen, but also at every moment of our lives, step after step, action after action. For a disciple of Buddha, there is no place in daily life that zazen does not fill. Zazen is not part, but all.

In the end, zazen means being concentrated on each action of our lives: when we eat, when we go to the toilet, when we sleep, when we go to bed – whether or not we go to bed alone. It is always with the mind of zazen. In the dojo, we are alone and not alone at the same time. It is the same with our relationship to alcohol, if we drink it. It is our duty to take care not to start spouting nonsense when we have been drinking. On this subject Master Deshimaru repeated over and over again that the disciple must be careful and correct. "Many of my disciples," he used to say, "follow this practice in the beginning, but then they let themselves go, or they simply become too familiar with things and they completely forget this attentive mind." So we must always, as far as possible, act correctly. Our attitude in life should not reflect *our* satori but *the* satori. It should express the infinite nature of Buddha.

I once read a newspaper review of a book on the modern Apaches[2] (Native Americans). It is interesting to see what interests people these days. In the final analysis I have the impression that they are interested in zazen, but without the structure that we have, without Buddhism. For example, the Apaches, adapting to modern times, explain that in a traffic jam, "You should straighten the back like a tipi." There is a photo of a Native American woman in the rear of a pickup, sitting up straight like a tipi. There are many additional observations. For example, "You should change your clothes after finishing work." It is the same in a dojo; we wear a kimono there, and one of the reasons for this is that it severs us from life in society, at least for an hour. But it is not just a question of a change of clothes; we wear the monk's robe to be able to withdraw, to abandon everything that is superfluous, everything that is decoration or social convention. Another suggestion of the Apaches is, "Throw your worries into the water!" The magazine quotes this example from the book: "Sit on the banks of the Seine, hold yourself straight like a tipi, figure out the direction of the current and throw your mix-ups and other furies into the water that is flowing and passing by."

That is *komyozo zanmai.*

...not only the* komyo *of the time of zazen. There is also the* komyo *that, step after step, action after action, gradually shows you that each phenomenon can be realized immediately...

This is truly the teaching of here and now. The *komyo* of zazen is simply the *komyo* of every step. Each step can be a step of *komyo* during zazen, every day, anywhere; this is the progress of *komyo*: body and mind become *komyo*. That is, the highest mind: the mind that is beyond. The highest-minded actions become *komyo*.

...each phenomenon can be realized immediately, automatically...

This can be understood intuitively. A thing can be actualized immediately if it is neither thought nor non-thought. We could also say, "Do not dwell on phenomena." Our lives are difficult enough without us adding extra weight to phenomena. The heavier that phenomena become (as, for example, in extreme affluence or, on the contrary, complete material destitution), the less freedom or free mind exists. Many Zen expressions capture this concept of "each phenomenon realized immediately." For example, "One thing becomes all things," or "Real life is always now."

...independently of your own understanding and your personal thoughts.

60

So, step after step, do not take anything for personal consciousness. Step after step, do not identify anything as being your own consciousness. Master Ejo already talked about this in a previous paragraph, saying that we must not display any pride in relation to the teaching of our master. Here again he advises us not to depend on our own understanding, as for example when we say, "I know what Buddhism is; I understand Zen." This is not true, anyway. It is impossible to "know" Buddhism or Zen.

I like the master's observation on this subject very much: "Do not seize any opportunity and do not set any goal."

Such is the true and authentic certification that exists without disturbing the expression of komyo.

Without disturbing the expression of the light of zazen, the light of *hishiryo*. Each step becomes *komyo* and can bring happiness and freedom. It is just a question of doing zazen, this practice that illuminates without being committed to any goal. So let's not go from thought to thought. And in order to avoid that, let's first be aware of being seated with a slight tonus that continues during zazen, during *kinhin*, and after zazen. Otherwise we will continue to go from thought to thought until we die. And all will be lost.

It is the spiritual power of non-acting in the light that illuminates itself. This komyo is originally non-substance, non-existence. This is why, even if many buddhas realize it in this world, they are still not of

> **this world. And being in nirvana, they are however not there either.**

> **...the spiritual power of non-acting in the light that illuminates itself.**

This is the light that lights up by itself and does not depend on the power of the mind – either yours or ours.

> **...even if many buddhas realize it in this world, they are still not of this world.**

Or, in other words, even when buddhas appear in this universe, the light does not appear. Nor does it enter nirvana when buddhas enter nirvana – that is to say, when they die. Why? Because even then, the light of awakening does not leave us. It does not abandon us.

Though it is subtle and difficult to comprehend, this is absolutely the thought of Zen. The light does not appear "at the right moment," at least in Zen, or at any specific moment, and it does not disappear either, "at the wrong moment" or at any other moment. *Komyo*, the light, awakening, does not move. It does not have the quality of coming or going. There is, in the end, neither outside nor inside. This is also why, when a monk asked Master Joshu if a dog has buddha nature, Joshu replied, "*Mu*," meaning nothing, among other things.*

In this section, Ejo is speaking of the present moment.

---

* How could "buddha nature" be *here* rather than *there*? And how could it be possible that this "buddha nature" could even be *in the dog* in the first place?

Here is a poem by Master Menzan, "He is an old hermit with white hair." In this poem, white hair symbolizes those who have ceased to enter into conflict with themselves and who have no more ambitions; hermitage is a word that implies zazen.

He is an old hermit with white hair.
His hermitage is in a deep valley.
He goes out and makes his way
to the market in the little town
And mingles freely with the crowd.
He does not come any more than he goes.
Buddha becomes like a child.

At the hour of your birth, komyo *was not in existence.*
At the hour of your death, it will not disappear.
From the point of view of the buddha-state, it does
not increase.
From the point of view of the senses, it does not diminish.

At the hour of your birth, komyo *was not in existence.*
At the hour of your death, it will not disappear.

This means without coming and without going. Of course, the body dies, but not the mind, not the *hishiryo*, consciousness. The mind of *hishiryo* remains. The mind in question is the storehouse (*zo*) of this light. And this mind, although called "storehouse," is not located *here* rather than *there*, or *there* rather than *here*. Nor is it located in any particular place in the cosmos.

> **From the point of view of the buddha-state, it does not increase.**
>
> **From the point of view of the senses, it does not diminish.**

For example, when the United States bought Alaska two hundred years ago, the country became bigger, but not the world. The world did not change at all; it did not grow a millimeter by this acquisition. We could say the same thing about the ego. Why? Because it is *ku*, empty. Our practice is therefore not to abandon the ego, the little me, but to free ourselves of it – rejecting and integrating are two very different things.

Our life is connected to the whole cosmos and that is what Ejo is talking about here. But our life is not limited by our birth and our death; it is not something personal, individual. In order to better free us of this ego, the Zen master tries to make us understand that in the end, there is no separation. For a Westerner, this is not so easy to accept, because it concerns a different idea of God than the Christian idea of a separate entity.

Master Deshimaru often talked about "finding the normal condition again." The normal condition is non-separation. The Zen master tries to have us consider all things in their entirety. On the level of phenomena, energy is changeable, yet in truth, it neither increases nor decreases. And that is what Ejo is telling us: the state of buddha, like *komyo*, did not appear at our birth and will not disappear at our death.

Just as when you have illusions or doubts you cannot ask the right question, when you have satori, you cannot say so.

If you are in illusion, obviously it is difficult for you to ask the right question. That is why *mondos* are important, because there we ask our question not only in front of the master but also in front of the whole group of practitioners, which requires us to be precise.

If you are awakened, how will you explain it? How will you explain it with your mouth, in front of everybody?

The practice and *satori* are not separate: this is a fundamental teaching in Soto Zen. Awakening is illumination, *komyo*. *Komyo* shines alone and everywhere; it is beyond the mind, beyond all sensation, all visualization. We cannot see this illumination even though it exists.

Those who transform their karma (that is, there where causes are produced) can become truly free. All Buddhists, monks, nuns, bodhisattvas of both the Mahayana and Hinayana are deeply marked by the image of Shakyamuni Buddha sitting beneath the Bodhi Tree. They never ask, "What is he doing sitting there?" Well, he is transforming his karma. Although he is completely motionless, he is not at all passive; he is completely active, "in action." Transforming one's karma is a long and difficult process, but it is very active.

So how do we express it? Ejo says that this cannot be expressed, at least in language. He writes, *you cannot ask the right question... you cannot say so.* Indeed, those who live in illusion cannot ask the right questions, and those who are awakened cannot say so.

Yet the two are not separate. For illusion becomes awakening and awakening becomes illusion. The Masters often repeat, *bonno soku bodai*: illusion becomes *satori*. However, they don't so often say, *bodai soku bonno*: awakening becomes illusion. And yet, *bodai soku bonno* is also true...always be aware of that.

Just as when you have illusions or doubts you cannot ask the right question, when you have satori, you cannot say so.

In the end, we cannot count on language. We hear this very often in Zen texts. For example, Sosan talks about it in the *Shinjinmei*; and in the *Hokyo Zanmai*, the *Sandokai* and the *Gion Shogi*, Tozan, Sekito and Fuyo Dokai say it too.[3]

The invisible world cannot be explained or expressed through language, this is true; yet there exist many Zen writings and dojo teachings, both from past times and from the present day. For words can be effective if they come from the non-personal, from the non-self, and if they are listened to and heard by the non-self.

Moment by moment, do not consider anything according to your personal consciousness. Twenty-four hours a day, you should be as calm and supremely tranquil as the dead. Do not think of anything by yourselves. Thus, from breath to breath, your profound nature, like your sensory nature, will unconsciously, naturally become non-knowing, non-understanding.

This means the same thing again: do not follow your thoughts. If we do not fall into knowledge, into classifications and their complications, our life can become like the current of a river. At all events, we must "go back" into the water, "go back" into the current, find again the river that is without beginning or end. And entering this current is done through zazen practice.

For all twenty-four hours a day, Ejo tells us, be as peaceful as the dead, as a corpse. To practice zazen is to enter the coffin. It is to lose our little being, the one that is ambitious, anxious, egoistical. To enter the coffin is to say goodbye to all that, once and for all.

To become completely calm again is the beginning of the practice. If you do this from one breath to the next, you will reach *man sho*, that is to say, hearing and touching the nature (*man*, to achieve or reach; *sho*, nature). "Hearing the nature" does not mean listening to the little birds! It is simply hearing, neither *for* nor *against*; it is hearing the not-two. It is becoming not-knowing, non-conceptual, where the body and mind are in perfect unity. Then there is no more ego to pull us down, down towards our pettiness.

To come back to not-knowing, non-discrimination, non-separation is to come back to that which is universal. For that we say, "It is not necessary to have a goal." It is *mushotoku*. For if we have a goal, separation appears; discrimination, classifications, the good and the bad, all appear. And the little "me" appears…

From that point, everything can naturally become calm, the radiance of komyo, *in the unity of body and mind. That is why when we call it, it has to reply quickly. It is the one and only* komyo *that harmonizes the people of* satori *and the people of illusion in one whole. So even if you start moving, the movement should not disturb you. And the forest, the flowers,*

> **the blades of grass, animals, human beings, all phenomena – be they long, short, square or round – can be realized immediately, automatically, independently of your personal understanding and the personal activity of your thoughts.**

This paragraph is not very difficult to understand, but we need to come back again to the meaning of the word *komyo*: the light of samadhi, the light of *mushotoku*, the light without object, the light of no-goal. Being naturally calm, in the unity of mind and body, is nothing other than the radiance of *komyo*.

When somebody calls us, we answer without hesitation, without creating any space between the question and the answer. Whether it is a question of the forest, flowers, blades of grass, animals or human beings, all is realized, immediately. And be they long, short, square or round, all phenomena are manifest immediately, without personal thinking, *independently of your personal understanding and the personal activity of your thoughts.*

This reminds us of the beginning of the *Komyozo Zanmai* where it says: *without being influenced by your personal understanding.*

In this section, Master Ejo demands a lot from disciples, as in fact, do all the other paragraphs of the *Komyozo Zanmai* that speak deeply to us of what the practice of zazen may bring. He shows us the method for being calm and patient when external events become apparent, when the ten thousand phenomena fall on our heads, at work or in times of unemployment, and in all the moments of our daily lives. On the subject of our disagreements and, on a more emotional plane, our family problems, Ejo offers us solutions that we can implement with our bodies and our minds.

That is why when we call it, it has to reply quickly.

Or immediately – it's the same thing. This means without hesitation, just as we put one foot in front of the other when we are walking in *kinhin*.

There exist many kinds of hesitation and even of non-hesitation. In Japan, at Eiheiji temple, I saw the monks respond instantaneously when they were called by the person responsible for their *samu*. The moment that the monk in charge called them, they would come running from all directions to present themselves to the leader, forming a line in front of him and standing to attention! But this is not what Ejo means by, "You must reply rapidly." In fact, Ejo is talking here about the light of *komyo*, which is not gradual but sudden. Why is it sudden? Because it is a matter of the primordial activity of our hypothalamus.

Then Ejo says:

So, even if you start moving, the movement should not disturb you.

Master Sosan discussed this question in his *Shinjinmei*, composed in the 7th century (Ejo's *Komyozo Zanmai* was written in the 13th century). It tells us of the tranquility that becomes movement.* In zazen, you are tranquil, without any apparent movement, the spine straight, the chin tucked in, the stomach appeased. But here come the *bonno* reappearing – that is, the movement of thoughts. I find this very accurate and the first time that I heard this sentence from

---

* Line 11 of the *Shinjinmei* says, "If we stop all movement, the mind becomes tranquil, and this tranquility then causes movement once again."

the *Shinjinmei*, it greatly helped me to understand movement and non-movement, high and low, coming and going.

In the first few years of the practice, we try to correct the "bad" by going towards the "good," but constructing scaffolding in the head like this ends up going wrong. We say to ourselves, "I've been practicing for two years, five years, every day, and yet I am not progressing at all." This is always the case. For example, if we do something good – like writing a book – we then want it to be appreciated, to sell well. This is no longer *mushotoku* but *ushotoku*, having a goal.

It is the opposite of the Mahayana way, the way that we practice, the middle way, the way that Ejo indicates to us – like all of the masters of the transmission. It is not a question of whether or not we are progressing, but simply of not following our thoughts. This doesn't mean behaving like a robot, but exactly the opposite: not being driven by phenomena, by this or that, because by going from thought to thought we will only find ourselves trapped against the railings in the end. As has been said, not going from thought to thought, nor from non-thought to non-thought, is the great freedom of mind and body.

Do not become attached to clothes, nor to food, nor to your home. Do not succumb to sensual desire or to the attachment of love, which are like the activity of animals. There is no point asking others about komyo, *because their* komyo *cannot be of any use to you.*

How do we dress, how do we eat? We each have our own ways. And why not, if that doesn't disturb anyone else? This said, we should not worry about what others are doing.

Do not succumb to sensual desire...

Personally, I wouldn't have wanted to follow a master who had never felt any sexual desire. I cannot imagine a master, a patriarch, Bodhidharma, Buddha, who never felt sexual desire. But they are simply not attached to it. It is the same with attachment to love. If we do not reject attachment to love, says the master, then it will reject us.

Do not become attached, Ejo tells us in this short paragraph. In other words, do not become attached to all of that. Do not come down on one side or the other. Do not come down on the men's side; do not come down on the women's side. Do not remain on it; do not dwell on what is relative or exclusive.

There is no point asking others...

It is useless to discuss what is good and what is not, or to talk about the pretty clothes in a shop, the good food at a restaurant, or the house with its great veranda. Do not succumb to attachments of this kind.

Ejo wrote this text for his disciples. That is why he talks like this: don't do this, don't do that. But in reality, there is no "don't do this, don't do that"; it is just a question of paying attention, being vigilant, having a good posture in zazen. When we become a monk or nun we wear the *kesa* or the *rakusu*. We chant the *Bussho*

Kapila and then we eat *genmai*, and this is how all our actions can become actions of *komyo*.

There is no point asking others; that cannot be at all useful. It is a question of being alone, face to face with oneself. No need to talk to others about our *komyo*, our light, our awakening. The practice is secret, hidden, so as to protect it better, contain it better. It is in our body, without goal, without words.

At its origin this samadhi is the holy dojo, the ocean of all the buddhas. It is therefore the greatest and most holy of all the seats transmitted directly from buddha to buddha through the holy universal practice. Being disciples of Buddha now yourselves, you should do zazen peacefully on his seat.

This section lauds the dojo, the place of practice, of *satori*, of awakening. We do not often hear a place of practice spoken of so majestically. Of course, each time that we think of the dojo in its original sense, we are thinking of Buddha seated beneath the Bodhi Tree. But since that time, the word dojo has extended in all directions.

Ever since the beginning, this *komyozo zanmai*, this samadhi, is the dojo, the place where Shakyamuni reached awakening; since that moment, it represents all dojos where meditation is practiced. It is *the ocean of all the buddhas.*

This paragraph puts the emphasis on zazen, on sitting, the practice of the buddhas, which has been transmitted to us exactly from generation to generation. It is *the greatest and most holy of all the seats*. It is the seat of Fuyo Dokai's *Gion Shogi* and of Master Deshimaru's *Bukkoku Zenji*. It is the seat transmitted directly from master to master, from buddha to buddha, from Buddha's disciple to Buddha's disciple—from disciples to disciples by means of zazen, the universal practice, that which is in touch with all existences. The *Komyozo Zanmai* is this, too.

Now that Ejo is approaching the end of his text, the only one that he wrote in his life, we can see that his tone is becoming a little more dramatic, even urgent. "You, my disciples," Master Deshimaru used to say, "you must become true monks and nuns, not professional monks and nuns. True monks and nuns must help others by means of their practice, not through words." In a profound sense, Deshimaru was not somebody who talked a lot. His commentary ends thus: "You must behave as a true guide on the path, a true master." Ejo, for his part, says, "a true saint." And at the end of this penultimate part, he reminds us that we must never forget, not even for a moment, that we are all children of Buddha.

Do not sit on the infernal zafu, the zafu of the gaki, animal or asura, nor on the zafu of the shomon or the engaku. And do not practice anything but shikantaza. Do not waste your time. This is what is known as the authentic spirit of the dojo and the true komyozo samadhi, the marvelous and splendid satori.

In Okamura's version of the *Komyozo Zanmai*, one of the best known other existing version, it says, "Never sit down behaving like a demon." You can see for yourselves the different visions, the different approaches to the teaching, Okamura's, Deshimaru's...

Ejo is talking here about the different paths on which we may be led astray. *Gaki* is desire; *gaki Zen* is the Zen that seeks the personal satisfaction of a goal. *Asura* is the path of aggression. *Shomon* is the moralist, like those who cultivate their personality and so become narrow and limited. *Engaku* is one who seeks *satori* for him or herself. *Engaku shomon* refers to those who practice in solitude for their personal illumination. But in certain texts and other translations of the *Komyozo Zanmai*, there is reference instead to *shravaka*, the kind of practitioners among whom Gautama Buddha was numbered, also defined as those who are seeking ways to escape *samsara*. Master Nyojo said of them that, even though they are not led by desires, they lack compassion.

The essence of Zen practice is to reduce egoism. Yet even if we understand that egoism is something to be freed of, it is very difficult to disentangle ourselves from it because all of our upbringing has been focused on developing it. And if things continue in this way, it is possible that one day the whole of humanity will disappear, ceding its place to other species.

In any case, freeing oneself from the ego does not only influence oneself but all existences – that is certainly why we practice zazen, *shikantaza*. And that is also *komyozo zanmai*, the light of *mushotoku*.

For me, Master Ejo's extraordinary text concludes here. The two short paragraphs that follow function rather as an epilogue, needing no commentary.

This text should only be read by true disciples of Master Dogen, those who have permission to enter his room.

I have written it for my zazen companions so that they will not hold mistaken points of view, as much to improve myself as to educate others.

Appendix

SOTO ZEN LINEAGE TRANSMISSION CHARTS

A brief overview of several Soto Zen lineages of distinction in the West regrouped by transmission of the teaching (*I shin den shin**) rather than by official certification.

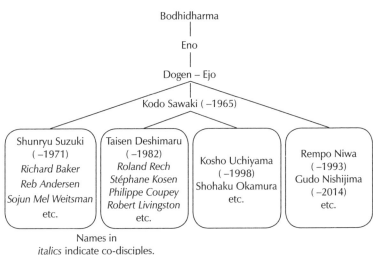

Names in *italics* indicate co-disciples.

---

* *I shin den shin*, literally from "mind-to-mind" or from "heart-to-heart." This has nothing to do with the official certification as indicated in most other genealogical charts to date, but solely with the master-disciple transmission.

Appendix

THE RINZAI-SOTO LINEAGE

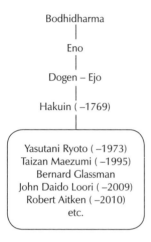

Bodhidharma
|
Eno
|
Dogen – Ejo
|
Hakuin (–1769)
|

Yasutani Ryoto (–1973)
Taizan Maezumi (–1995)
Bernard Glassman
John Daido Loori (–2009)
Robert Aitken (–2010)
etc.

Please note: These charts show only a few of the many lineages in the West. Of the lineages mentioned, we have focused on certain important disciples we know. For further details about the Kodo Sawaki-Deshimaru lineage, please consult our website: *www. zen-road.org*

Endnotes

PREFACE
1. Bernard Faure, Dôgen, La vision immédiate, Le Mail, 1987.
2. From *To You*, a compilation of sayings of Kodo Sawaki that can be found at: http://antaiji.dogen-zen.de/eng/kodo-sawaki-to-you.shtml

PART I
Sansho Doei
INTRODUCTION
1. Daichi Sokei (1290-1366). A whole series of poems by Daichi is dedicated to the samurai Kikuchi entitled, "Teaching to the samurai Kikuchi."

COMMENTARY ON POEMS
ONE
1. The first poem of the *Eiheikoroku* by Master Dogen:
   Mujo Seppo, the wordless sermon:
   The wordless sermon of the *Tathagata*,
   Who can understand it?
   A stick made from the branch of a tree understands it unconsciously.

   And the second poem:
   Mid-June teaching to my disciples:
   We must lead ourselves by our own nose-ring.

During the three months that summer lasts,
we persevere in the practice.
Today there are only thirty days left.
So we must increase our efforts
and put out the fire burning on our heads.

TWO

1. *What words can express the inexpressible beauty?*
Joseph Needham (1900-1995), a historian of Chinese science
wrote, "Buddhism has never lost its characteristic of refusing to give
answers to questions that it considers pointless because they concern
things that are impossible to know."

FOUR

1. From Namkhai Norbu Rimpoche, *Dzogchen and Zen*, Nevada City,
CA: Blue Dolphin Publishing, 1984.

FIVE

1. These commentaries have been published as a book in French: *Mon
Corps de Lune*, éditions Désiris, 2007.

NINE

1. This was the great debate among intellectuals and dropouts in the
United States and France in the 1960s, and I plunged right into
the middle of it. It was the time when everybody was talking about
William Burroughs, Timothy Leary, Richard Alpert, alias Ram
Dass (whom I had met in person), the pioneers of the psychedelic
movement, and in Burroughs' case drawing his inspiration from
what are known as hard drugs. Burroughs also presented himself as
being familiar with Buddhism. "For the West," he wrote, "Buddha
is simply history to be *studied*. It is a subject to be *understood*. But
I repeat, *Buddhism is not for the West*. We must develop our own
solutions." And he adds, "Buddhism often boils down to nothing
but a mountain of psychological shit." He considered that Buddhism

was finally nothing more than another psychedelic drug – a little like Marx calling religion "the opium of the people," which, of course, is not the case. The writer and critic Dana Wilde writes that William Burroughs did much to tear down the moral structures that led to the world wars and the atrocities of the 20th century "and I think we must forgive him his own corruptions in gratitude for his sacrifice."

At this time and in this circle, although we talked about the *doors of perception* (a famous study by Aldous Huxley on the mind-expanding effects of LSD and mescaline, among other drugs) and the state of mind of the sage, we knew nothing of Zen monks and nuns. But gradually, as time went on, we turned toward the drugs that were used in certain master-disciple relationships: Castaneda's peyoti, hashish for certain Indian gurus (sadhus), and so on. It did not occur to us that there might be other psychological practices that we had not yet encountered, whether chemically based or not. Of course, we heard talk of Zen meditation, yet we did not really associate it with a state of mind that was "beyond," a state of mind of inner revolution. We thought that meditation was part of the religion of Eastern priests.

Everyone was always wanting to find something, and not only in an effort to satisfy our desires. However, what we were finding was never the "real thing." And many of us ended up in prison, where the real thing was not found either.

And anyway, what is the real thing? Perhaps it is the Way, awakening; the inner joy that one cannot express to others. Love – we must each decide for ourselves what is the real thing. Master Deshimaru told us, "It's as you like. Thus we taste the deep meaning of things." And we reach "the marvelous bliss."

What is the real thing?

I do not know. It's nothing. But this nothing, even in the most difficult moments that we may live through, is there. The without-object.

PART II
Komyozo Zanmai
COMMENTARY

1. According to the religious authorities in China, these caves of Dunhuang were looted in the early 20th century when they were discovered by European archeologists.

2. The article was *"Les six ruses d'indiens apaches."* [*The six tricks of the Apaches,*] (Le Parisien, 13/09/2007).

3. Line 73 of the *Shinjinmei* by Master Sosan: "Here the way of language breaks down, there is no more past, present or future."

    From the *Hokyo Zanmai* by Master Tozan: "Our consciousness is not language..." and, "Flustered by words, you will fall into an abyss."

    From the *Sandokai* by Master Sekito: "Receiving this language, you must understand its source..."

    From the *Gion Shogi* by Master Fuyo Dokai: "The second patriarch, Eka, stayed out in the snow and cut off his left arm; that was really tough. But Bodhidharma didn't say a word about it, and Eka didn't say much either and didn't ask a lot of questions. They understood each other completely, from mind to mind."

Glossary

A

Arhat (Skrt., Pali, *arahat*, Jap., *rakan*). A saint who has reached the highest level on the Hinayana path, the "smaller" vehicle. Unlike the bodhisattva of the Mahayana who wishes to save all beings, the *arhat* is mainly concerned with his or her own salvation.

B

Bodh-Gayâ. A village located not far from the Bodhi Tree, beneath which Shakyamuni Buddha had his awakening. The supreme holy place for Buddhists.

Bodhidharma (Jap., *Bodaidaruma* or *Daruma*, 470-543 CE). Bodhidharma was the twenty-eighth patriarch in the lineage counting from Buddha and the first Chinese patriarch of Zen, the disciple of the Indian master Hannyatara and the master of Eka. An Indian monk from Sri Lanka, he spent the last decade of his life in China, where he died at the age of 150. When he arrived in China by boat in 520, he held a brief but famous *mondo* with the emperor, then left to head north, towards the Yangtze River. After traveling for thousands of miles on foot, Bodhidharma reached the northern mountains where he occupied a cave that would become the temple of *Shorinji* on Mount Suzan (in Chinese, *Shaolin* on Mount Sung). Known during his lifetime as "the brahman who faces the wall" he remained, according to legend, seated in his cave facing the rock wall for nine years.

Bodhi Tree. *Bodhi* means "awakening" in Skrt. The tree beneath which Shakyamuni Buddha experienced awakening at the end of forty-nine days of meditation. According to tradition, this tree was an *assattha* or *pippala* (*ficus religiosa*), recognizable by its heart-shaped leaves.

Bodhisattva (Skrt.). "Awakened being, living buddha." A human or celestial being who incarnates the ideal of the Mahayana. Unlike the *arhat* of Hinayana Buddhism who is consecrated exclusively to his own salvation, the bodhisattva has made a vow to save all beings before reaching his (or her) liberation.

Bonno (Jap.). *Bon* means that which disturbs; and *no* means that which causes suffering or that which torments. *Bonno* is usually translated as "passions," although this term is much too restrictive. The *bonno* are our illusions, our attachments, everything produced by our personal consciousness.

Bonno soku bodai (Jap.). "Illusion becomes *satori*."

Bussho Kapila (Jap.). The name of the mealtime sutra, after the first line of this sutra, *Bussho Kapila,* meaning, "Buddha was born in Kapila." It is sung in temples before *genmai* and lunch, but not dinner, since the Buddha did not eat after the middle of the day.

D

Daichi Sokei (1290-1366). Japanese Soto Zen master well known for his poetry. He received monk ordination from Kangan Giin (1217-1300), a disciple of Dogen, and later practiced with Keizan for seven years. At the age of twenty-five, he left for China and stayed there for eleven years. Returning to Japan, he received transmission from Meiho Sotetsu (1277-1350), a close disciple of Keizan. Daichi, who had no successor, died alone in his temple at Kyushu that was later burned by the Jesuits. He remains famous for the many original poems that he wrote about zazen.

Deshimaru, Taisen (1914-1982). Disciple of Kodo Sawaki, whom he followed for 30 years until the master's death in 1965. Equipped only with Sawaki's kesa, bowl and zafu, he moved to Paris, where he spent the last 15 years of his life teaching Zen and establishing a large community of practitioners all over Europe and North Africa. He was one of the few Japanese Zen pioneers who came to the West not sent by a religious institution or other organization. Instead, he continued Kodo Sawaki's teaching in liberating Zen from clerical and hierarchical structures by putting the emphasis on zazen and the necessity to practice it in daily life. Deshimaru is also known for his calligraphies, his skills in martial arts and his translations of major classical Zen works. He died in 1982 from pancreatic cancer. His teaching continues today by his disciples and their respective sanghas at La Gendronnière in the Loire Valley, in Paris, and in most of the other European capitals, as well as in Montreal and New Orleans.

Dharma (Skrt., Pali, *dhamma*, Chin., *fa*, Jap., *ho*). A central concept of Buddhism used in several senses: The universal truth proclaimed by Shakyamuni Buddha, the teaching of Buddha, and Buddhist doctrine. "Truth, ultimate reality, the cosmic order, universal law." In this usage, the word dharma predates Shakyamuni Buddha ontologically, as well as all the buddhas of the past. Also, "phenomenon," as in the phrase, "However numerous the dharmas may be, I vow to master them all."

Dogen Zenji (or Dogen Kigen, Eihei Dogen, 1200-1253). Great Japanese Soto Zen master, disciple of the Chinese master Nyojo and master of Ejo. Much criticized in his time, he introduced Soto Zen to Japan and founded the temple of Eiheiji, situated in the mountains in the north. Born to a family of the upper nobility, he studied Rinzai Zen and *koan* method for many years with masters Eisai and Myozen. Then he crossed the sea to China where he met the Soto master Nyojo. He practiced by his side on Mount Tendo for three years before returning to Japan as heir to Nyojo's Zen. Dogen is the author of an authoritative work, the *Shobogenzo*, in which most of his teachings are found. His poems are collected in the *Sansho Doei*, with the exception of the poems of the *Eiheikoroku*.

Dogen's teaching essentially rests on three points:
- Practice without goal or object (*mushotoku*).
- Abandoning body and mind (*shin jin datsu raku*).
- Practice itself is *satori* (*shusho ichinyo).*

Dojo (Jap.). Also known as *zendo*. The place where zazen is practiced (*do*, the way and *jo*, the place). Originally, the place where Buddha attained *satori* (beneath the Bodhi Tree), the dojo is therefore a holy place. Dojos as we know them, appeared in China in the 7th century with the patriarchs Konin and Eno.

E

Eiheikoroku (Jap.). Collection of poems by master Dogen in ten volumes. These poems, brought together by Ejo after Dogen's death, remained secret and restricted to Dogen's closest disciples. Until 1672, they were transmitted by copying, when Manzan Dohaku finally published them.

Ejo (or Koun Ejo, 1198-1280). Dogen's principal disciple and secretary. Known for his loyalty to his master (whom he helped create a *sangha*), as well as for the historic work that he did in transcribing and compiling the *Shobogenzo*. Born in Kyoto to a noble family, he met Dogen in 1234 at Kosho-ji temple, became his disciple and stayed by his side until Dogen's death in 1253. Ejo was then inaugurated as the second abbot of Eiheiji. Despite being abbot in his own right, Ejo continued to be Dogen's disciple to the end. During the remaining twenty-seven years of his life, he stayed close to the tomb of his master and visited his room every day after zazen to light incense. At the end of his life, Ejo left instructions that his ashes should be buried beside Dogen's at the place reserved for the secretary.

Engaku (Jap., Skrt. *pratyeka-buddha*). "Achieved awakening by oneself." Originally, this term referred to a person who withdrew from the world and sought awakening in solitude in the forest. One who practices in order to be in good health and become a saint.

F

Fuyo Dokai (Chin., Furong Daokai, 1043-1118). Great Zen master in the Soto lineage. He refused the highest imperial honor, the purple kesa, in protest against the obligation of monks to pray for the emperor's long life. Thus he was exiled to Lake Furong situated in northeastern China. In opposition to the decadence of many Soto Zen teachers of the times, Fuyo Dokai insisted on food provided exclusively through the cultivation of gardens by the resident monks on the monastery grounds. He refused to accept invitations and beg. Hence, he would dilute the *genmai* (rice soup) with water to make it go further when excessive numbers of disciples flocked to his monastery. One attribute of his teaching is the importance of the continuity of zazen and *samu*. He is also remembered for his noted text, the *Gion Shogi*.

G

Gaki (Jap., Skrt., *preta*). "Ghosts" or "hungry spirits." Also, one of the six worlds (See *samsara*). In this state, one is consumed by insatiable desires for food, riches, power, and so on. In Zen monasteries, it is the custom to make an offering of a small part of one's meal to the *gaki* before starting to eat.

Gendronnière, La. Zen temple located in the Loire Valley, founded by Master Deshimaru in 1979. La Gendronnière is the principal temple of the sangha of Master Deshimaru's disciples. Niwa Zenji visited in 1984 to confer the *shiho* on three of Master Deshimaru's disciples. Besides the traditional two-month summer camp, La Gendronnière is above all a place of practice dedicated to *sesshins*, daily zazen and *samu*.

Genmai (Jap.). "Brown rice," literally, "rough rice." A rice soup eaten after morning zazen. This tradition, which continues today, dates from the time of Fuyo Dokai, who died in 1118. A simple dish for people who practice zazen and lead a simple life, *genmai* is made up of six ingredients: brown rice, leeks, celery, carrots, turnips and onions.

H

Hannya (Jap., Skrt., *Prajna*). "Wisdom." A central concept in Mahayana Buddhism signifying an immediate, intuitive wisdom, not an abstract wisdom that depends on the intellect.

Hinayana or Theravada (Skrt.). One of the two major branches of Buddhism, opposed to Mahayana. Theravada teaching puts its emphasis on following the *sila* – precepts – and the writings of the Pali canon. Its ideal is the *arhat*, the self-liberated sage. Today, Theravada is mainly found in Southeast Asian countries such as Sri Lanka, Thailand, Cambodia and Laos.

Hishiryo (Jap.). "Beyond thought." *Hi* means beyond and *shiryo* means thought. Thinking from the depths of non-thinking, beyond personal consciousness. With *shikantaza* and *mushotoku*, *hishiryo* forms one of the three pillars of the teaching of Kodo Sawaki and Taisen Deshimaru.

Hokyo Zanmai. (Jap.). "Samadhi of the Precious Mirror." This poem by Soto Zen master Tozan (died 869) is one of the four oldest texts of Zen, celebrating the true nature of all things. Seen by all masters as the expression of the essence of Zen. Recited in Zen monasteries in Japan, the *Hokyo Zanmai* is considered one of the fundamental texts of Soto Zen on a par with the *Shinjinmei*, the *Shodoka* and the *Sandokai*.

Hypothalamus. The instinctive, primitive central brain, as opposed to the rational, intellectual frontal brain. It is located in the lower rear part of the cranial cavity. It is seen as the point of union of body and mind.

I

I shin den shin. "From mind to mind" or "from heart to heart." A fundamental notion in Zen that describes the transmission beyond writing and intellectual understanding; the common intuition between master and disciple of reality as it is.

J

Joshu (Chin., Zhaozhou, 778-897). Great Zen master, disciple and successor of Nansen Fugen. Master Dogen called him "Joshu, the old buddha." During the last 40 years of his life, he taught and practiced with a small group of monks. Although he had thirteen successors, his line died out after a few generations probably due to the many wars and frequent purges of Buddhism in China at the time. Joshu is mentioned in many koans. He is also well known for the extreme poverty that he and his sangha lived in.

K

Kanji. Japanese characters, pictograms representing words or ideas, as opposed to *kana,* which represent syllables.

Karma (Skrt.). "Act, action." Law of universal causality. The totality of our actions and their consequences. Karma is created by the action of body, mouth and mind. Karma is the law of cause and effect, and from it comes transmigration and *samsara.* Karma encourages correct behavior based on being aware that behavior has an effect on the phenomenal world, rather than the observance of commandments or the expectation of either a reward in heaven or punishment in hell. Individual karma and collective karma exist, and both transcend birth and death. Through the practice of zazen, each of us influences the karma of all humanity.

Kesa (Jap., Skrt., *keshaya*). Large garment made of many pieces of carefully assembled fabric that Zen monks and nuns wear draped around their shoulders on top of the *kolomo*. Presented by the master at the time of ordination, the *kesa* is an object of faith and veneration. It symbolizes the transmission and membership of the uninterrupted line of Buddha's disciples, existence in a dimension that transcends the small ego.

Ketsumyaku (Jap.). Certificate given at the time of ordination that shows membership of the line of transmission and gives the names of all of the masters from Shakyamuni Buddha to the disciple being ordained.

Kinhin (Jap.). "Zazen in motion." Walking meditation to the rhythm of one's breathing, practiced during the interval between two zazens.

Koan (Jap.). Literally, "public case." A phrase, word, act or gesture that leads to understanding the truth. Can be used as a tool for educating disciples. Rinzai Zen uses *koans* as a technique with the aim of obtaining *satori*. Soto Zen, which does not attach value to particular states and identifies *satori* with the normal condition, does not use *koans* for training disciples. Nevertheless, for Soto (as for Rinzai), the *koan* represents the hidden, ungraspable side of reality.

Kolomo (Jap.). Black Zen monk or nun's robe distinguished from the kimono by its wide sleeves, worn over a white or gray kimono.

Kontin (Jap.). "When the mind sinks into torpor during zazen." The opposite is *sanran*.

Ku (Jap., Skrt., *sunyata*). "Emptiness." "Existence without substance." In Zen, the source of all things. Often translated as "emptiness" as opposed to *shiki*, "phenomena," yet a nihilistic view of the world is not to be understood in this. *Ku*, which means "sky," denotes the infinite, the unborn, from which everything that is born and finite arises, and to which it all returns. It is also the origin, the common identity in which differences (phenomena) do not exist.

Ku sokuze shiki, shiki sokuze ku. "Emptiness becomes (is) phenomena, phenomena become (are) emptiness."

Kusen (Jap.). *Ku* here means mouth and *sen* means teaching. "Oral teaching given in the dojo by the master during zazen." Teaching that directly addresses the *hishiryo* consciousness of practitioners, without passing through the intellect. "*Kusen* is neither literature nor a lecture. It should attack and impress the mind of the disciple. It should resonate with the deepest part of the brain and give rise to intuition and the highest qualities," explains Master Deshimaru. *Kusen* appears to be characteristic of the lineage of Masters Kodo Sawaki and Deshimaru. Most other lineages favor lectures (*teisho*).

M

Mahayana (Skrt.). "Great vehicle." One of the two branches of Buddhism, the one that includes Zen; the other is Hinayana ("smaller vehicle"). Mahayana appeared in the first century BCE. It stressed the vocation to save all humanity over and above one's individual salvation. This attitude is incarnated by the *bodhisattva*, an ideal character whose principal virtue is compassion (*karuna*). Mahayana took root mainly in Tibet, China, Korea and Japan.

Mayoi (Jap., Skrt., *maya*). "Illusion, deceptiveness, appearance." The world of phenomena, forms and appearances.

Menzan Zuiho (1683-1769). Zen master and well-known Soto scholar. Author of more than fifty works including biographies of Master Dogen and commentaries on his teachings. He sought to have the temples of his day revert to following the most orthodox patterns set up by Dogen, an influence that is still seen in Japan today.

Mondo (Jap.). A question and answer session between disciple and master held in the dojo for the benefit of the whole *sangha*. Many *mondos* have been recorded in the history of Zen for the edification of generations of practitioners.

Mu (Jap.). A particle of speech meaning "nothing," "nothingness," "none." "Nothing," yet not in the sense of "nothing" as opposed to "something." More than a negation, *mu* contains the connotation of absence. It is found in many Japanese expressions including *mushotoku* (non-profit), *mushin* (non-mind), *muga* (non-ego).

Mujo (Jap., Skrt., *anitya*). "Impermanence." A fundamental condition of all existence. The study of *mujo* is an essential aspect of the practice of the Way. Master Daichi wrote, "*Mujo* never stops watching you, not even for a moment, and when it strikes, it does it with such swift suddenness that you are struck down before you even realize what is happening."

Mushin (Jap.). "Without mind, without personal consciousness." A state that is free from dualistic thoughts.

Mushotoku (Jap.). "Nothing to obtain." Without goal or profit-seeking mind. *Mu* is the negating prefix and *shotoku* means to obtain or profit. *Mushotoku* refers to the practice without object or goal, the act of giving freely.

N

Nansen Fugan (Ch., Nanquan Puyuan, 748-835). Disciple of Baso Doitsu and master of Joshu Jushin, among many others. Seven years after the death of his master, he went into isolation on Mount Nansen where he practiced zazen for thirty years. Then he spent the last ten years of his life in a monastery, surrounded by more than one hundred disciples.

Nento (Skrt., Dipamkara). "The Torch Burner." Legendary buddha who stands for all of the buddhas of the past. According to tradition, he was at least 96 meters tall and lived for one hundred thousand years.

Nyojo (Chin., Tiantong Rujing, 1163-1228). Disciple of Setcho Chikan and master of Dogen; Soto master of the Sung dynasty. During his travels, he came into contact with all of the forms of Zen that existed at the time. Certain schools were mixing zazen with the recitation of the *nembutsu*, counting the breaths, Taoism and Confucianism; others with the study of *koans*. Saddened by this state of affairs, Nyojo became abbot of Tendo monastery in southern China and taught only zazen. A resolute opponent of "spiritual syncretism," he considered that the unique teaching of Bodhidharma had no need of additions or mixings. As for the monks who advocated such practices, he called them "corruptors of the true teaching" and "destroyers of the Buddha Dharma."

Nyojo was the last of the great Chinese Zen masters and it is only thanks to Dogen, who carried Nyojo's teaching back to Japan that it has survived to the present day.

R

Rakusu (Jap.). Small *kesa* worn around the neck, resting on the chest. It may be worn not only in the dojo but also in daily life. Unlike the big *kesa*, the *rakusu* is not restricted to monks and nuns; those who have received bodhisattva ordination can also wear it.

Rinzai school. Founded around the teachings of Master Rinzai in China in the 9th century. Today, Rinzai and Soto form the two main schools of Zen. Rinzai Zen places much emphasis on *kensho*, the experience of one's true nature. The practice leading to *kensho* consists of zazen, *koans* and *samu*. *Koans* are often used during zazen as a meditation object. Traditionally Rinzai education is rather martial or sharp (*zusan*), in contrast to *men mitsu*, the more delicate approach in Soto Zen education.

S

Samadhi (Skrt., Jap., *zanmai*). "Complete concentration, complete absorption of mind." State of non-duality, of pure concentration that is unconscious and without object. Master Dogen explained, "The samadhi of the buddhas and patriarchs is frost and hail, wind and lightning."

Samsara (Skrt., Jap., *shoji*). "The Wheel of life and death." The cycle of transmigration, the cycle of life and death that generates karma. The opposite of nirvana. Comprises the six possible modes of existence: *shomon* (human), *asura* (warrior), *deva* (god), *chikuso* (animal), *gaki* (starving spirit), *naraka* (the hells).

Samu (Jap.). "Sacred work." Activity of monks and practitioners for the benefit of the sangha: gardening, construction, cleaning, publishing teachings, and so on. Sometimes called "practice through work," or "the continuity of immobility and inner silence in activity."

Sandokai (Jap.). Poem written by Master Sekito Kisen in the 8th century. *San*: difference, *do*: similarity, *kai*: fusion. "The fusion of difference and similarity." One of the fundamental texts of Zen recited daily in the Soto monasteries of Japan, cited and commented upon by a great number of masters. The *Sandokai* ends with these famous words, "You who seek the Way, I beg you, do not waste the present moment."

Sangha (Skrt.). The company of monks, nuns and lay practitioners who follow the Way of the Buddha and practice together. One of the three treasures of Buddhism, along with the Buddha and the Dharma.

Sanko (Jap.). "Life in the mountains or the forest." The title of a group of poems in Master Dogen's *Eiheikoroku*.

Sanran (Jap.). State of excitement or mental agitation in zazen; the opposite is *kontin*.

Satori (Jap.). "Awakening, return of individuals to their true original nature." Illumination or awakening, brought about by means of fundamental cosmic power rather than the ego. *Mushotoku* brought to life. Not a special state of consciousness but a return to the normal condition. In the Rinzai school, *satori* is the culmination of a fruitful practice and is the object of a passionate quest. In the Soto school, the practice itself is *satori*; in other words, fusion with the natural order of things.

Sawaki, Kodo (1880-1965). Great Japanese Soto master of the 20th century and master of Taisen Deshimaru. Ordained by Koho Shonyu in Kyushu at the age of eighteen, he then studied with Shokoku Zenko. He spent most of his years shunning temple life to travel up and down Japan teaching Zen, which earned him the nickname "Homeless Kodo."

Sekito Kisen (Ch., Shih-t'ou Hsi-ch'ien, 700-790). Literally, "Stone Head." Disciple of Seigen Gyoshi and master of Yakusan Igen. Considered to be the first link in the chain of Soto Zen. Author of the *Sandokai*, one of the fundamental texts of Soto Zen. When he died in zazen at the age of ninety, his body mummified. The mummy can still be seen at Sojiji temple in Japan. One of his poems says,

> To the west of the river lived Baso.
> To the south of the lake, Sekito.
> People went from one to the other.
> Those who had not met them, lived in ignorance.

Sesshin (Jap.). "To touch mind." A period of several days dedicated to intensive practice of zazen and *samu*.

Shikantaza (Jap.). "Simply sitting" without goal or object. The seated posture that encompasses the whole universe without using techniques like *koans* or counting the breath.

Shiki (Jap.). "Consciousness." Phenomena, as opposed to *ku*, emptiness. The phenomenal world.

Shiki sokuze ku, ku sokuze shiki (Jap.). "Phenomena become (are) emptiness, emptiness becomes (is) phenomena."

Shinjinmei (Jap.). *Mei*, collection for the benefit of others. *Jin*, faith. *Shin*, heart, mind. Poem about faith in zazen by Master Sosan (died in 606), the third patriarch. Composed in the 5th century CE, it is the oldest known Zen poem.

Shobogenzo (Jap.). *The Treasury of the Eye of the True Law*, Master Dogen's magnum opus, partly compiled by his disciple Ejo. It was the first great Buddhist work written in Japanese; a dense text of inexhaustible richness that recapitulates and develops all the teachings that Dogen received in China. Not content with "following in the footsteps of the masters of bygone days," Dogen also improvised on traditional themes, demonstrating great freedom of mind and an impressive virtuosity.

Shodoka (Jap.). "Song of Immediate Satori" or "Song of Awakening" by Yoka Daishi (665-713). The second most important *Chan* poem after the *Shinjinmei*, sixty-eight verses long, it begins:

Friend, do you not see
This man of satori has ceased to study and to act?
He does not push away illusions, nor does he seek the truth.

Shogun (Jap.). "General." From 1192 to 1867, the title of those who held both military and civil power in Japan.

Shomon (Jap., Skrt., *shravaka*). "Listener." In Mahayana, *shomon* refers to disciples who aspire to personal illumination. Corresponds to the stage of the *arhat*.

Shoshin (Jap.). "Beginner's mind." "Fresh mind."

Sosan (Chin., Seng-ts'an, d. 606). Third Zen patriarch and author of the *Shinjinmei*. Almost nothing is known about Sosan's life except that he was a disciple of Eka and master of Doshin. He died upright in *kinhin*.

Sutra. Discourse given by Buddha. According to tradition, the sutras were compiled from memory by his disciple Ananda at the First Buddhist Council that met in 480 BCE, just after the death of Shakyamuni. They usually begin with the words, "Thus have I heard."

T

Tozan (or Tozan Ryokai, Chin., Tung-shan Liang-chieh, 807-869). Zen master, author of the *Hokyo Zanmai*, "The Samadhi of the Precious Mirror." Disciple of Ungan Donjo and master of Ungo Doyo, among others. Co-founder, with Sozan Honjaku, of the Soto school.

Z

Zafu (Jap.). Round cushion filled with kapok (a silky fiber obtained from a tropical silk-cotton tree) upon which one sits to practice zazen; Buddha used dry grass. Raising the seat off the ground allows the spine to straighten correctly. There is a famous Zen saying, "You must first die on the zafu."

Zazen (Jap., Chin., *ts'o chan*). *Za* means "to sit." Sitting on a zafu with legs crossed and back straight, facing the wall in the Soto tradition and facing the center in the Rinzai tradition. The breathing is slow and deep, and the mind observes thoughts without following or fueling them. (See *hishiryo, mushotoku, shikantaza* and *shin jin datsu raku*.)

Index

Index

Index of ZEN Stories

Books by the Author in English

ZEN CLASSICS:

Zen Simply Sitting. Chino Valley, AZ: Hohm Press, 2007. [Commentary on *The Fukanzazengi* by Master Dogen.]

In the Belly of the Dragon, Vol. 1. New Orleans, Louisiana: American Zen Association, 2005. [Commentary on *The Shinjinmei* by Master Sosan.]

BOOKS BY TAISEN DESHIMARU, COMPILED AND EDITED BY PHILIPPE COUPEY:

Sit: Zen Teachings of Master Taisen Deshimaru. Chino Valley, AZ: Hohm Press, 1996. [Teaching on education in Rinzai and Soto Zen.]

The Voice of the Valley: Zen Teachings. Indianapolis, Indiana: Bobbs-Merrill, 1979. [Forthcoming by Hohm Press in 2015.]

Zen & Budo. Paris, France: Budo Editions, 2014 [Teaching on the link between Zen and the martial arts.]

WORKS OF FICTION:

Horse Medicine, New Orleans, Louisiana: American Zen Association, 2002. [Alias M. C. Dalley].

Temple Rapidly Vanishing, France: Deux Versants Éditeur, 2012. [Alias M. C. Dalley.]

About the Author

Philippe Coupey, Zen monk, was born and raised in New York City. After studying literature, he took an unusual series of jobs, including uranium prospector, housepainter, social worker and translator. In 1968, he settled in Paris. Four years later he met Zen Master Taisen Deshimaru with whom he practiced zazen. He quickly became one of Deshimaru's closest disciples, working on his master's translations and teachings. Three books came out of this collaboration: *The Voice of the Valley: Zen Teachings* (Bobbs-Merrill, 1979), *Sit: Zen Teachings of Master Taisen Desimaru* (Hohm Press, 1996) and *Zen & Budo* (Budo Editions, 2014).

Ordained as a monk, Rei Ryu Philippe Coupey followed his master until the latter's death in 1982. Since then he has continued to work and teach within the International Zen Association that Master Deshimaru founded.

Today, he is one of the principal Soto Zen teachers in Europe in a lineage that is directly transmitted from master to disciple and whose practice is *shikantaza*: simply sitting, without goal or profit-seeking mind.

For more information on Philippe Coupey's Sangha in Europe, please contact:

Sangha Sans Demeure
6, square de Port Royal
75013 Paris
France
www.zen-road.org

For information on American Zen Centers in the Deshimaru lineage, please contact:

American Zen Association
New Orleans Zen Temple
748 Camp St.
New Orleans, LA 70130
www.nozt.org